MONT-BLANC

SKI TOURS

MONT-BLANC

SKI TOURS

Eric **DELAPERRIÈRE**
Journalist and Photographer

Franck **GENTILINI**
Mountain Guide

Le Vieux Servoz - 74310 SERVOZ - FRANCE

Acknowledgements
We would like to thank all those who have helped us with this book, by their information, suggestions, corrections and criticisms.
Our thanks to Xavier Dunand, Jean-Pierre Cane, David Cumming, Hubert Bessat, Philippe Chillet, Gilles Tahon, Luc and Catherine Louise, Sophie Revel, Olivier Michel, Jean-Paul Demargne, Jean Pierre Mansart, Philippe Deylard, Guy et Jerôme Semet, Jean Marc Tamborini, Sylvie Kunz, Philippe Chirinian, Rémy Lecluse, Caroline and Glenn Watters, and everyone else that we might have forgotten.

Translated into English (of sorts) by Dave Lovage, part time sportsman, part owner Chef of the Alchimie Bar-Restaurant, Rue Vallot Chamonix.

Cover: Frank Gentilini, Patrice Labarbe

WARNING TO THE READER

This book has been written in the touring or climbing guide's alpine tradition. It is written for well-informed and responsible skiers who are aware of the risks involved when they leave the prepared slopes. Despite all the precautions taken to avoid any errors or misunderstandings in interpretation, the authors do not claim to be infallible. They therefore decline all responsibility for any accidents which could befall the readers using this book.

The descriptions of the itineraries however precise they may be, cannot replace a true knowledge of the terrain. The mountain landscapes can change from year to year depending on the snow levels, snow drifts caused by the wind, avalanches or changes in the forest layouts. The quality of the snow may make certain usually very safe slopes dangerous for several days. This quality can only be fully understood by looking at the evolution of the weather conditions throughout the season.

For the occasional skier, the city dweller or the foreigner from the other side of the world who comes to spend just a few days in the Alps, it is nevertheless necessary to hire a high mountain guide or ski instructor neither of which this book aspires to replace.

EQUIPMENT

Here, we are only talking Alpine ski touring equipement, although telemarking has seen something of a rebirth these last few years.

Skis

Most of the large manufacturers have some touring skis in their catalogue with their distinctive hole in the spatula, very useful for hoisting or making an emergency sled. These skis are generally easy to control in all snow conditions, close to what we call "compacts". If they can satisfy beginner to intermediate skiers, good skiers may be disappointed with their performance at higher speeds and their holding ability on hard snow. For them it is better to use an off piste ski.

There is of course, the recent emergence of new ultra light skis, coming from the ski- mountaineering competitions. These we reserve for long tours, or light people.

Ski maintenance is very important as snow conditions vary. Sharp edges and waxed bases are indispensible. We recommend "O-Sixo" for the bases, which is compatible with seal skins. Wax your skis regularly with an iron, so that the wax penetrates into the base, scrape them well, then do a few runs before fixing your skins on.

Bindings

These have two essential characteristics, to fix down or release the heel, to go respectively down or up.

They are also made with the same safety devices as a normal alpine binding, but these are not as efficient.

Some have ski brakes, but this is not too important as we prefer powder leashes, which make putting your skis on on steep slopes easier. All bindings have heel lifts to raise your foot angle on steeper climbs, taking the strain off your calves.

Also there is the Secura-fix or Alpine trekker bindings which clip into alpine bindings. Useful only for short tours.

Boots

These are a cross between a ski boot and a mountaineering boot: plastic shell, 2-4 buckles, a Vibram sole to help walking and climbing. Several makes share the market, some are made for lightness and comfort, whilst others put the accent on rigidity for the downhills. Certain models possess specific inserts for use with ultra light bindings, take note when you buy your equipement.

Poles

Ordinary poles will do, although telescopic poles are better on long traverses (we shorten the uphill pole), or where you have to carry everything (poles in sack).

Skins

Happily these are no longer made of seals skin, nowadays they are mohair or synthetic. They are sticky, we stick them on for the way up, and take them off on the way down. Correctly dried and folded, they should always be ready for the next climb. Particular care must be taken to: never dry them in direct heat (sunlight, fire etc), dry them after each use and regularly renew the glue (after peeling off the old). Fold carefully after each use.

They should be 10 cm shorter than your skis.

The heel end should be bevelled to minimalise unsticking, the width should leave your edges clear, otherwise you will have no traction whatsoever when traversing on hard snow.

In case of repeated unsticking during the route, several solutions exist:
- Wrap strong tape around both ski and skin.
- Use a quick setting spray on glue and leave it to dry a bit before resticking.
- Use double sided tape.

If too much snow sticks to your skins, making progression difficult, you can use another spray called "Mohair" to reduce it.

Harscheien

These are metal blades, either fixed or mobile, under your bindings, depending on the make. Each system has its defenders; the fixed ones are safer and permit the use of heel lifts while the mobile ones make advancing easier but are not much use with heel lifts.

Take them on every route, especially with parabolic skis.

Rucksacks

The model to use, and its set up, depends on the usage envisaged: 25-40 litres for a one day route, a minimum of 45-60 litres for routes of several days, more if you have to carry sleeping bags, cooking equipement etc...

Take a solid sack with ice axe fixings and lateral straps for skis (a small strap to attach ski tips is useful), a waist belt and, less essential, a chest strap. Avoid walking rucksacks with side pockets as these make ski carrying difficult.

Clothes

Use preferably a multilayered formula as this enables you to easily adapt to different temperatures and effort levels. Synthetic underwear and long sleeved t-shirts (avoid cotton which doesn't dry easily). One or two fleeces of differing thicknesses, Gortex or similar overclothes (jacket and trousers or salopettes). One-piece ski suits are not much use for ski touring except when its very cold. Balaclavas, bonnets and a peaked cap (to keep the ears warm and sun out of your eyes).

Pay particular attention to your gloves, take at least two pairs, light leather or fleece for the climbs and a thick, warm, waterproof pair of mittens. Silk undergloves for the real cold.

Glacier quality sunglasses are a must, and a ski mask for bad weather or wind.

Avalanche tranceiver:
Peeps, a small transmitter/receiver for avalanche victims, using a standard frequency (457 KHz). Always to be carried in the transmission position and worn permanently from the start of the route. Wear it where you cannot lose it. This locates buried skiers through a sonic signal and directional light diodes. **Training in their use is highly advisable and can be obtained from the various clubs and guides organizations.**

The snow shovel is the obligatory companion to the peeps; Each member of the group must carry one, it is stupid to take only one per group as is too often the case, especially when we know that its use increases the chances of survival of the victims (by 90%).
Nowadays, lightweight modeles (500 grm) exist. Also they can't be beaten when it comes to rapidly building an emergency shelter.
In the same fashion **snow probes** and **survival blankets** should be part of individual equipement.

For tours on glaciers
The harness and **the rope** are indispensable. Recent models of harnesses with adjustable leg straps and high rope attachment points are perfectly adapted for ski touring.
The rope is very useful on technical passages (ridges, exposed slopes etc...)
A sensible idea would be for every member of the group to carry a small rope (30m of 8,5 mm is a reasonable compromise).

In order to be able to get out of a crevasse on your own, or rig up a pulley, each skier must be equiped with an **ice screw** (hand screwable), **3 loops of 5mm rope**, 1m50 long, and/or **one or two autoblockers** (jumar or ropeman), a sling step, 2 or 3 screwgate **carabiners** and a 9 mm short rope attached to the harness and the top of the rucksack by a screwgate (to tie on in a crevasse if the harness is not accessible).

On the more technical routes a few more ice screws, slings, a snow anchor, and a few rock pitons would not go amiss.

And of course you'll need an ice axe and crampons.

Don't forget the **First aid kit**, with bandages, aspirin, anti-inflammatory cream etc...

The **Compass, altimetre,** and the **map**, preferably 1/25000, are necessary in case of fog or sudden bad weather.

As with the A.R.V.A. it is better to learn how to use them properly before you set out.

Repair kit

Very useful for on the spot repairs of rucksacks, skis, bindings etc... A small pair of multi use pliers, two flat spanners of 8 mm and 10 mm, two screwdrivers, one flat and one solid no. 9 phillips or posidrive (test it on your bindings), and a few spare screws of all relevent sizes. Add a tube of cyanolite glue, some steel wire, some screw rivets to repair boots and a sewing kit.

THE DANGERS OF SKI TOURING

Ski touring allows you to adventure in high and medium mountain terrain on snow, in winter but above all in spring. The difference between this and ski resorts is the army of ground crew who try to take out anything dangerous, even going as far as filling in crevasses.

In ski touring the risks are always present.

It is each person's responsibility to study and adapt their chosen route, depending on conditions, and to be capable of turning back if it seems wise to do so.

Avalanches

The major risk in ski touring. These occur when the snow mantle unbinds itself from its bottom layers and starts to flow under the influence of gravity. There are several types:

- **Powder avalanches** are the most dangerous. They generally occur after a fresh snowfall. Powder forms a spray which can move at considerable speeds (up to 300 km an hour), generating an intense blast wave.

- **Slab avalanches** are caused by the collapse of compact snow slabs. These are formed near ridges or cols, most often on the leeward side of the slope. They can last a long time after fresh snow and be recovered by subsequent snowfall. This makes them difficult to detect. If you set one off, try to ski out sideways. Same if one is set off above you.

- **Wet snow avalanches** are due to the softening of the snow, after prolonged exposure to the sun or warm air, and have the advantage of being a lot slower than the others. But, at the end of the season, they can attain gigantic proportions and go right down to the ground, ripping out blocks of ice, rocks, and trees. Avoid them by crossing potential risk areas as early as possible in the morning and looking out for old avalanche paths.

In all cases, if forced to cross a risk zone, we adopt a few simple rules: Unstrap the waist and chest belts of your rucksack, take off your powder leashes, take your hands out of your pole loops, dress well (zips done up, long sleeves, and gloves), keep a minimum of 25 m between skiers and don't stop before reaching a sheltered spot. Advance one by one between sheltered areas, cross the risk zone as high as possible or, even better, make a detour (if possible) by a ridge.

EUROPEAN SCALE OF AVALANCHE RISK

for the information of the public using the mountains away from marked, open trails

Risk index	Snowpack stability	Probability of triggering
1. Weak	The snowpack is well stabilised on most slopes.	Triggering of avalanches is only possible on a very few steep slopes (*) especially if heavily overloaded (***). Only small avalanches and snowslides occur spontaneously.
2. Limited	On several (**) sufficiently steep slopes, the snowpack is only moderately stabilised. Elsewhere, it is well stabilised.	Triggering of avalanches possible, especially if heavily overloaded (***), on some slopes whose characteristics are generally described in the bulletin. Spontaneous avalanches of any size are not to be expected.
3. Pronounced	On many (**) sufficiently steep slopes, the snowpack is only moderately to poorly stabilised.	Triggering of avalanches possible, sometimes even if slightly overloaded, on many slopes whose characteristics are generally described in the bulletin. In certain situations, some spontaneous medium sized, sometimes fairly large, avalanches are possible.
4. Strong	The snowpack is poorly stabilised on most (**) sufficiently steep slopes.	Triggering of avalanches possible, even if slightly overloaded (***), on most sufficiently steep slopes. In certain situations, many spontaneous medium size, sometimes large, avalanches are to be expected.
5. Very strong	Generalised instability of the snowpack.	Numerous large spontaneous avalanches are to be expected, including on terrain that is not very steep.

(*)   Slopes particulary prone to avalanches, because of their gradient, ground configuration, proximity to a ridge...

(**) The characteristics of these slopes are generally explained in the bulletin: altitude, aspect, topography...

(***) Overloading code =
   - **heavy**: for example, grouped skiers...
   - **slight**: for example, isolated skier, pedestrian...

The term "triggering" concerns avalanches caused by overloading, in particular by skiers.

The term "spontaneous" concerns avalanches which occur without external action.

Crevasses

These result from the continuous movement of the glaciers under the effect of annual snowfall, which thickens their tops and causes a natural flow towards the valley. Their speeds can reach several dozen metres a year. Where the slopes break up or change direction or angle, pressures are created which crack the ice and form crevasses. We learn to recognize these pressure zones and to avoid them, but this can be difficult after fresh snow so we have to guess where the crevasses are by the form of the new snow. If the route passes areas which we know to be highly crevassed, for example: "la Jonction" under the "Grand Mulets", we ski roped up, by twos or threes, on the way up as well as the way down, which calls for good co-ordination between skiers. The bergschrund is the "last" crevasse which marks the limit between the glacier, which moves, and the mountain faces, which don't. Cross it as fast as possible at what seems to be the safest point. It is sometimes possible to jump it on the way down, but make sure the landing is steep enough.

Avoid taking off both skis on a glacier and keep well dressed.

If you do fall in, try to secure yourself with an ice screw to prevent yourself from falling deeper in.

Falling Seracs

These are balanced slices of glaciers which break off and fall under the pressure of the movement behind. We avoid as much as possible passing under them.

If you cannot avoid doing so, the faster you go the better.

Take a good look first at where you have to cross. If you see small pieces of blue ice this means some have recently fallen here. Remember that it is the forward movement of the glacier which causes the falls, temperature changes and time of year play a very small role, so they can fall at any moment.

Bad weather, fog

Always check the weather forecasts, by telephone and in the daily bulletins posted in most resorts and police stations.

If you are caught out in sudden bad weather, the best thing to do is to turn

round and follow your tracks back out. If they have disappeared, you will need your compass, map and altimetre, which means knowing how to use them...
Be especially careful in very thick fog, perceptions of distance, angle and time change dramatically, stop frequently to check.
If you are caught in a storm and lost you must dig a shelter.
Building an igloo is complicated, we prefer a trench. Dig it out to about 1 m 50-2 m deep by 2 m-2 m 50 long and 50 cm wide (snow shovel). Half way up cut out 50 cm high sleeping alcoves, cover the top of the trench with your skis, survival bag, snow blocks and anything else you have spare. Leave a small space for air. The temperature in this type of shelter will stablilize around 0°, and one candle will raise the temperature by 2 or 3°, not bad when it is -25° outside ! Cover each bench with a survival blanket, put on all your clothes and sleep with your feet in your rucksacks. Never sleep in the bottom of the trench, you could be asphixiated by your own carbonic gases. The bottom part serves as a trap for these gases, as well as a sump for the cold, the warmth rising up.

Technical difficulties

Certain passages such as some steep slopes, bergschrunds or passages on rock, mean using a rope: We put in place a fixed rope from a belay (anchor). The first person crosses the obstacle, then sets up another belay for the second etc... If in doubt don't hesitate to use this manoevre, it takes up some time but better safe than sorry... There are several possibilities for anchor points: a sling around a rock spire, pitons, nuts, friends, ice screws, etc... Most often though we have to use a snow anchor of some sort. We can drive a pair of skis as deep as possible, crossed over, into the slope. This is the quickest way but a safer belay can be had by digging a trench, 50-70 cm deep, across the slope, in which you place a pair of skis or another "deadman", an ice axe for example. Attach a sling to the middle, then fill in the trench before attaching the rope. This is the best belay for exposed descents or places where you'll put a lot of weight on the rope. You can then go down with the rope around your shoulders, either sideslipping on skis or on foot with the skis on your sack. If it's really steep, use a descender.

In case of accident

Inform the rescue services as soon as possible by radio, mobile or the nearest place you can find with facilities. One reason why it's better to tour in groups of at least four. One can stay with the injured party while the others go for help. Whilst waiting cover the victim, make sure they are not in direct contact with the ground and if possible place them somewhere with easy access for the rescue services.

For first aid it is essential that at least one of the group has taken a course.

Club Alpine Francais

For 350 FF a year you get very good insurance cover and reduced refuge prices.

MOUNTAIN HUT

Most refuges are permanently open but aren't always manned during the winter season. For the ones that are, you are required to reserve in advance, especialy at the weekends or bank holidays.

In the "winter hut", the part of a refuge always left open, you will often find blankets and mattresses so a sleeping bag isn't always necessary. But what is available varies greatly from refuge to refuge. In the Swiss refuges you will generally find a wood burning stove or a gas burner, as well as cooking utensiles and plates. Everything necessary for a pleasent stay! In France and Italy, unfortunately, luxuries like this are rare so carry a small cooker.

For more information contact the refuges directly, or the clubs which look after them.

Please do not forget to pay for your stay by slipping an envelope in the box provided.

Before leaving, fold up your blankets and close all the doors and windows, a little thought for those that come after you.

ROUTE DESCRIPTIONS

Access

Indicated where it is not obvious, to help you find the nearest town or village to your route. These are described at the beginning of each regional presentation.

Starting point

The beginning of your route, the side of a road, a carpark, or the top of a ski lift.

Height difference

The vertical height difference "up" is the total of all the climbs made, and the same for the vertical height difference "down".

Orientation

Information on the principal orientation of the slopes to be encountered. This is important because of the following: north facing slopes stay longer in the shade and so keep their powder longer. South facing slopes are quickly exposed to the sun and it is much better, and safer, to get past them early to avoid slush and avalanches.

Degrees of difficulty:

The following grades have been made assuming hard but not frozen snow. They can vary greatly depending on the prevailing conditions.

We have also decided to divide the graduations between the climb and the descent.

For the upward parts we will use the classic terminology as follows.
- **VE: VERY EASY.** Corresponds to large gentle slopes and snow covered paths with few or no step turns.
- **E: EASY.** For slightly steeper slopes with perhaps some narrow passages, where step turns are easy, even for complete beginners.
- **SD: SOME DIFFICULTY.** Narrow or sustained 30° slopes where certain step turns could be delicate for inexperienced skiers.
- **D: DIFFICULT.** This indicates slopes of 30 to 40° with kick turns demanding a cool head and a reasonable amount of experience. It may be necessary to walk in places.
- **VD: VERY DIFFICULT.** Climbs of 40 to 45° which we would generally make with our skis on our rucksacks.

we will add "**+**" for courses which vary between two categories.

The descents. For the downhill parts of the routes we will use the Blachere scale, with some small modifications. This seemed pertinent to us because it defines for each degree the required level of technical and mental competence.
- **IMS:** Intermediate skier. Someone who has mastered stem christies, kick turns and can sideslip on slopes of up to 25 or 30°.

- **GS:** Good skier. Knows how to safely deal with all types of snow on slopes which can be steeper than 30 to 35° and where certain passages can be narrow and delicate.
- **VGS:** Very good skier. Capable of technical jump turns on slopes of up to 40° and having the qualities of self control necessary to turn in a narrow couloir where a fall would be serious.
- **EGS:** Extremely good skier. All the previous qualifications, plus an excellent technique and a solid mental control on slopes of 45° and over, where the commitment is total. This is extreme ski territory.

An **A** will be added for routes requiring a minimum of mountaineering knowledge: abseils, short rope work, pulleys. Use of crampons, ice axes and ice screws for mixed routes and glaciers.

Important

Just because you have been down a short 45° gully in a ski resort, doesn't mean you are ready to confront one of the real 45° faces in the high mountains.

Timing

For the time given ascending, we have kept to an average of 300 metres per hour, adjusted in accordance with the distance and difficulty of technical passages (fixed ropes etc...). The time given to descend is not so easy to determine because it largely depends on snow conditions and the capabilities of each skier. Therefore a reasonable margin has been allowed.

All technical manoeuvres can take more time than expected. Also the number of participants must be taken into account.

Time of year

Always check local weather conditions before setting out. Pleasant surprises are not generally the rule in the high mountains! Occasionally a sustained period of foehn (a warm south wind) can make spring routes practicable at the beginning of winter.

Equipment

Concerning the mention "tours on glacier" see page 10.

Itinerary

We have described as precisely as possible these routes but up to date maps, and knowing how to read them is a must. Wherever we could we have used marked photographs, however this is only a general indication. Always take into account local conditions!

Remember that the expressions, **the left bank of and the right bank of, correspond to the direction of flow** and are the same for a stream as for a glacier.

Other directions are to be taken in the sense of your progression and are often accompanied with geographical orientations.

The right bank of a glacier is the right-hand-side looking down but the left-hand-side looking up.

LES CONTAMINES
SAINT-GERVAIS

Situated in the far west corner of the Mont Blanc chain, les Contamines Montjoie sector is perfect for ski touring. It is in a wild setting, preserved by the nature reserve. There we can find all aspects of ski touring; from day trips with ski lift access, to ski mountaineering on glacial terrain.

Acces
8 km after St Gervais les Bains.
By car: Autoroute Blanche, Paris-Geneva-Chamonix, or by Albertville and Megeve on the RN (no tolls).
By train: SNCF St Gervais-Le Fayet, then the bus from the station carpark.

Lodgings
Numerous hotels and apartments, trailer park.
Ask at the tourist office: tel. 04 50 47 01 58.
CAF, mountain huts tel. 04 50 47 00 88.

Mountain huts:
Informations: refuges CAF: tel. 04 50 53 16 03
other mountain huts: Tourist office, tel: 04 50 47 01 58.

- **Refuge de Tre-la-tête (1970m)** private, manned in spring, no winter dormitory, tel. 04 50 47 01 68.

- **Refuge des Conscrits (2600m):** CAF, 80 places, manned in spring (15th March), winter dormitory 16 places, tel. 04 79 89 09 03, emergengy telephone.

- **Refuge Durier (3367m):** refuge bivouac CAF, 24 places, not manned but always open in ski season, gas cooker, emergengy telephone, tel. 06 81 10 94 76.

- **Refuge de Miage (Plan Glacier):** private, 25 places, unusable in winter. Emergengy telephone.

- **Refuge de la Col de la croix de Bonhomme (2440m):** 113 places, always open, unmanned in spring, gas, wood, kitchen utensils, tel. 04 79 07 05 28, emergengy telephone.

- **Robert Blanc (2750m):** private, always open, unmanned in spring, wood, kitchen utensils, tel. 04 79 07 24 22, emergency telephone.

- **Tête Rousse (3162m)**: CAF, 57 places, always open, unmanned in spring, tel. 04 50 58 24 97, emergengy telephone.

- **Gouter, (3817m):** CAF, 120 places, always open, unmanned in spring, tel. 04 50 54 40 93, emergency telephone.

- **La Balme Chalet Hôtel (1706):** private, a winter room without blankets, unmanned during the ski season, emergency telephone.

Ski lifts

Most of the routes in this sector can obviously be done from the bottom, especially from Notre Dame de la Gorge, but we have chosen to present them from the top of the lifts to put the emphasis on the descent. The day or weekly ticket is good for all the lifts in the ski area.

Useful addresses.

- Tourist office: tel. 04 50 47 01 58, fax 04 50 47 09 54.
- Guides' Office: tel. 04 50 47 10 08.
- Ski lifts: tel. 04 50 47 02 05.
- Weather service: tel. 08 36 68 02 74 or 08 36 68 10 20, minitel 3615 meteo.
- Train station Le Fayet: 04 50 78 23 46. Timetables: 08 36 35 35 35.
- SAT bus: 04 50 78 05 33.
- Taxi: 04 50 93 61 47.
- Mountain rescue: 04 50 78 10 81.
- Ski rental: Ronchail Sports 04 50 47 00 26.
              Mermoud Sport 04 50 47 04 46.
              Simond Sports   04 50 47 03 99.

Starting points.

1) Chairlift de la Buche Croisee:

From Contamines Village to Notre Dame de la Gorge, take the telecabine of the same name then the gondola Signal and ski down the red piste "the Gentianes" to the telesiege de la Buche Croisee, which will take you to the north-west ridge of the Aiguille de Roselette.

2) Notre Dame de la Gorge:

As above, but continue to the church at the end of the road (there is a large carpark 200 m before the church). This will allow the purists to start routes 1 to 7 from the bottom.

3) Le Cugnon:

Contamines Village, direction Notre Dame de la Gorge, after 500 m turn left towards the hameau du Cugnon (parking Tre-le-Tête).

4) La Frasse:

From the Contamines Village centre take the road which climbs up to the hameau de la Frasse (parking next to the road).

5) Bionnay-Le Champel-Bionassay:

From St Gervais, direction Les Contamines, after a few kilometres turn left to Bionnay and then right to Le Champel.

For Bionnassay, as above but after Bionnay take the left road to its end. (The carpark is just above the hameau de Bionnassay after the houses of "Crozat").

These roads can be pretty poor in winter, in which case start the routes from Bionnay.

6) Le Baptieu.

From the center of the Contamines go towards the "hameau du Lay" and park at the chairlift de Montjoie, otherwise carry on to the top of the "hameau de Baptieu" where the snow clearing stops.

1 - "COL DE LA FENETRE" (2245m)
(circuit)

Easy access from the ski lifts, no difficulties climbing, and a lovely downhill run through the nature reserve.

- Map   : IGN TOP 25 3531 OT Megeve
- Access   : Les Contamines
- Starting point : Chairlift de la Buche Croisée (Notre Dame de la Gorge)
- Height difference : 200 m up, 1040 m down
- Orientation   : up west, down east
- Difficulty   : E - IMS.
- Timing   : up 1-1hr30, down 1-1hr30
- Time of year   : December to April
- Equipment   : crampons for the walk out at the bottom.

- **Itinerary** (photo 1)
  From the Contamines village center, direction Notre Dame de la Gorge, park in front of the chairlift "de la Gorge". Take this one, then the chairlift "le Signal" and ski down the red piste "The Gentianes". Go up the chairlift "de la Buche Croisee". At the top go down the "Hautluce" side by traversing to the left underneath the "Aiguille de Roselette" to a large flat shelf. Climb up east until you see a rock barrier in the middle of which is a short, steep, narrow snow gully. This gives access to another shelf. Continue to climb towards the ridge between the "Aiguille de Roselette" and the "Tête de la Cicle". Reach the "Col de la Fenêtre" by moving well back left near the top (signpost at the Col).

- **Descent** (photo 2)
  Go down the steep but short slope then cross to the right under the "Tête de la Cicle". Follow the series of small valleys to the left of the obvious moraine until you reach the "Chalets de la Balme". From here take the path on the left which brings you, after a large flat area, to the edge of the forest. Take the road which cuts down through the forest, over a stone bridge and follow the "Voie Romaine" (Roman road), which is well marked and brings you back to "Notre Dame de la Gorge". The cross-country tracks to the left of the road enable you to arrive back at the lift.

- Safety tips:

Do not ski too fast on the Roman road, watch out for walkers, and especially the rocky drops to the side. The bottom part can be very icy and crampons could be useful here.

→

Photo 1:

1. Col de la Fenetre
2. Rochers des Enclaves traverse
3. Col des Chasseurs
4. Col des Chasseurs
4a. Col des Chasseurs - variant

2 - "LES ROCHERS DES ENCLAVES" (2465m)
(circuit)

O ne of our favourite routes in this sector. Superb view of Mont Blanc. A gentle easy climb with few step turns and a friendly ski down.

- Map : IGN TOP 25 3531 OT Megeve
- Access : Les Contamines
- Starting point : chairlift of "Buche Croisée"
- Height difference : 380 m up and 1215 m (plus 810 m on piste) down
- Orientation : north
- Difficulty : VE-IMS
- Timing : up 3hrs, down 1hr - 1hr30
- Time of year : December- April.

- **Itinerary** (photo 1)
  From Contamines Village, direction Notre Dame de la Gorge, park in front of the gondola station. Take this lift, then the "Signal" gondola, ski down the red piste "les Gentianes" and take the chailift de la Buche Croisée. At the top go down the "Hautluce" side by traversing to the left underneath the "Aiguille de Roselette" until you reach a large flat shelf (2050 m). From here, go southwards, traversing under the buttresses of the "Tête de la Cicle". Climb the gentle slopes which take you up to a broad rise (really a continuation of the southwest ridge of the "Tête de la Cicle"). Continue south-west following the crest of the rise and climb a short steep hillock. You can now reach the "Col de la Gitte" by a short descent. Rejoin easily the "Rocher des Enclaves" by following an obvious ridge south-west.

- **Descent** (photo 1)
  From the summit, go the same way down at first then, just before the "Col de la Gitte", go straight on following the large shoulder which dominates the "Lac de la Girotte". Around 2000 m this forms a left hand elbow and from here you will see some electricity pylons. Follow these to the "Chalet du Berger" (1778 m), then descend slightly right into the top of a fairly steep valley. At the bottom cross the stream by the bridge below the "Chalets de

Colombes". Depending on the snow, you now have two possibilities:
- 1: If the snow cover is good traverse through the forest to the red "piste de la Ruelle", go down it and take the chairlift up, then take the chairlift "du Col" to arrive at the "Col du Joly".
- 2: If the snow cover is poor climb out by the top section of the "Ruelle". From the "Col du Joly" use the green piste "Route du Col" to the "Signal", then the blue "De Montjoie", and finally the red "Retour Gorge" to get back to the carpark.

Tip: don't miss the last ski lifts!

3 - COL DE LA CICLE (2377 m)
(TRAVERSE)

A good climb/descent ratio, opposite the Domes de Miage.

- Map	: IGN TOP 25 3531 OT Megeve
- Access	: Les Contamines
- Starting point	: Teleseige de la Buche Croisee
- Height difference	: 325 m up, 1250 m down
- Orientation	: west then south east up, north-east then east down
- Difficulty	: E-GS.
- Timing	: Up 2hrs, down 1hr30-2hrs
- Time of year	: December to April
- Equipment	: Crampons for the walk out at the bottom.

- **Itinerary** (photo 1)

From Contamines Village to Notre Dame de la Gorge. Park at the gondola station. Take it, then the "Signal", and go down the red piste the "Gentianes" and go up the chairlift "de la Buche Croisee". From the top go down the "Hautluce" side by traversing to the left underneath the "Aiguille de Roselette" until you reach a large shelf (2050 m). Put on your skins and go southwards alongside the buttresses of the "Tête de la Cicle" to the bottom of its south-west ridge. Go round it by a steep traverse to the side which brings you to a flat area. Reach the "Col de la Cicle" by climbing a short valley.

→

Photo 2:
1. Col de la Fenetre
3. Col de la Cicle - traverse
4. Col des Chasseurs - traverse
5/6. To Col du Bonhomme et Tête nord des Fours
7. to Pointe sud des Monts Jovets

Col des Chasseurs

Col la Cicle

La Voie Romaine and Les Contamines

- Descent (photo 2)

From the pass go over the cornice, (sometimes tricky) and ski down the 30-35° slope. This shallows out considerably at the bottom. Work over to the right and follow the small valley between the moraines. Keep crossing right till you see the Chalets de la Balme, which you will reach by easy slopes. From here take the path to the left which brings you, after a large flat section, to the forest entrance. Take the route which crosses the forest, over the stone bridge, and follow the Voie Romaine back to Notre Dame de la Gorge.

- Safety tips

The slope used to get around the south west ridge of the "Tête de la Cicle" is short but steep. Keep your harscheisen on if the snow is hard.

4 - COL DES CHASSEURS (2530m)

One of the best descents in section, the climb on the "Cicle-Chasseurs" ridge is superb.

- Map   : IGN TOP 25 3531 OT Megeve
- Access   : Les Contamines
- Starting point : chairlift de la Buche Croisee
- Height difference : 450 m up, 1350 m down
- Orientation   : West up, North down
- Difficulty   : D-VGS-A
- Timing   : 3-4hrs up, 2-3hrs down
- Time of year   : December to April
- Equipment   : Crampons for the walk out.

- **Itinerary** (photo 1)
  As for n° 3 to the "Col de la Cicle". From there climb the steep slope to the right, scattered with rocks, which takes you onto the Cicle Chasseurs ridge (rope and crampons sometimes necessary). After climbing a short passage on easy rock, re-descend 40 m on the south west side. Follow the ridge, traversing the steep slopes, then a short descent will bring you to the col des Chasseurs.

- **Descent** (photo 2)
  From the col go up slightly to the right underneath the "Aiguille de la Pennaz" to go around the cornice (often imposing). Attack the couloir (40° at the top) which shrinks at first, then gets wider and shallower the closer you get to the Chalets de Balme.
  As for n° 3 back to the carpark.

- Variation

It is possible to reach the col de la Cicle by traversing directly the south-west ridge of the Tête de la Cicle, crossing several steep, narrow gullies. The rope is sometime useful, hence the A for alpiniste.

- Safety tips

This is an impressive descent, often in powder, with the associated avalanche risks. The cornice (sometimes impassable) is a good indication of snow accumulation.

→

Photo 3:
5. Col du Bonhomme
6. Tête Nord des Fours
6a. Tête Nord des Fours-descent-variant
7. To the Pointe Sud des Monts Jovets

5 - COL DU BONHOMME (2329m)

A fairly easy tour which takes you to the historic passage between the Val Montjoie and the Beaufortaine.

- Map : IGN TOP 25 3531 OT Megeve
- Access : Les Contamines
- Starting point : chailift de la Buche Croisee (Notre Dame de la Gorge)
- Height difference : 720 m up, 1600 m down
- Orientation : after the Col de la Fenetre north east
- Difficulty : E-IMS
- Timing : 3-4hr up, 1hr30-2hrs down
- Time of year : December-April
- Equipment : crampons for the walk out at the bottom.

- Itinerary (photos 2 and 3)

As for n° 1 to the Col de la Fenetre, after the Chalets de la Balme (1800 m approx.), skins on to climb across under the Aiguille de la Pennaz, in the direction of the pylon (subject to large avalanches after warm periods or heavy snow). Above the pylon climb the flatter area towards the south east. Around 2000 m you will come up against a small slope bordered to the right by a rocky gorge, go over the top of this to access the valley dominated by the large slopes coming down from the Tête Nord des Fours. Climb the last steep passage which takes you up to the Col de Bonhomme (shelter).

- Descent

By the same route back to the Chalets de la Balme, then as for the Col de la Fenêtre tour (n° 1) back to the carpark.

- Variant

Forget the lifts, do it from the bottom!

- Safety tips

Avoid this route in winter, when subject to the avalanche conditions stated above, and in spring when its too warm. The traverse to the EDF pylon is exposed to avalanches coming off the Aiguille de la Pennaz.

6 - THE TETE NORD DES FOURS (2556 m)
(circle)

A long tour with a descent down a narrow couloir, steep but not excessively so.

- Map   : IGN TOP 25 3531 OT Megeve
- Access   : les Contamines
- Starting point   : chairlift de la Buche Croisee
- Height difference : 1150m up, 2020m down
- Orientation   : North then south-west up, north-west down
- Difficulty   : E-VGS
- Timing   : 4-5hrs up, 2-2hrs30 down
- Time of year   : January-April.

- **Itinerary** (photos 2 and 3)
As for n° 4 to the Col de Bonhomme. From the pass continue by traversing upwards to the left on the south-west slope, direction Col de la Croix de Bonhomme. Before the col you will see a cairn, climb up a vague valley to the left (N.E). Go under the high tension cables and carry on to the Col des Fours (2665 m). Climb the summit ridge to arrive easily at the Tête Nord des Fours.

- **Descent** (photo 3)
From the top ski down the length of the north-east ridge on the Chapieux side. Just above the point marked 2708 m a pass marks the start of a lovely steep couloir (40° N-W side). Ski down this (a rope may be useful at the top) then down some gentle slopes, staying mainly to the right, to avoid the rocky outcrops, to rejoin the route around 1900 m.

- **Variants**
You can ski down the north-east slope at several other points on the ridge, notably from near the pylon.

7 - LA POINT SUD DU MONT JOVET (2362m)

To discover two lakes sleeping under the snow, at the foot of Mont Tondu.

- Map	: IGN TOP 25 3531 ET St Gervais and OT Megeve
- Access	: Les Contamines
- Starting point	: chairlift de la Bûche Croisee
- Height difference	: 735 m up, 1620 m down
- Orientation	: south
- Difficulty	: E-IMS
- Timing	: 3-3hrs30 up, 1hrs30-2h down
- Time of year	: December-April
- Equipment	: Crampons for the bottom.

- **Itinerary** (photos 2, 3 and 4)
As for n° 4 to the Col de Bonhomme as far as the flat area after the pylon. Go to the left (N.W) near the Chalets de Jovet at 1930 m. Keep climbing the gentle slopes to the north-east, staying well to the right of the stream coming down from the lakes. Then crab slightly to the left to join the south ridge of the Pointes de Jovet. The first summit is the Pointe Sud.

- **Descent** (photos 2, 3 and 4)
Same way down to the Chalets de la Balme, then as n° 1.

- **Variation** (photo 6)
Descent of the Combe Blanche: instead of climbing the Pointe Sud, you can carry on along the right bank of the lakes to the end of the valley. Around 2480 m climb onto the ridge coming off the N.W ridge of Mont Tondu. Ski down the steep slopes (40° VGS) of the small valley of Nant Blanc to join the Combe Blanche (1650 m). Cross over to the left to avoid the impassable cascade of the Combe Noir to reach the Hameau de la Laya and return by the Voie Romaine.

Pain de Sucre
du Mont Tondu

10a

7a

Pointe Sud
des Jovet

7

to la Balme

Good snow conditions are required to ski the couloir. This can be seen from the Signal chairlift arrival station.

- Security tips

Do not go too close to the lakes at the beginning of the season. You'll be skating on thin ice!

←

Photo 4:
7. Point Sud des Monts Jovets - 7a. Acces to the Combe Blanches descent
10a. Variant of descent Mont Tondu

8 - TETE DE LA COMBAZ (2455m)
(return trip)

A great classic, which can also be done from the Contamines or the Saint-Nicolas de Véroce ski lifts. This gives you a very good climb: descent ratio.

- Map   : IGN TOP 25 3531 OT Megeve
- Access   : Les Contamines
- Starting point   : Le Baptieu
- Height difference : 1270 m up and down
- Orientation   : South-East
- Difficulty   : SD-GS
- Timing   : 4 - 4hrs30 up, 1hr30 - 2hrs down
- Time of year   : January-March.

- Itinerary (photo 5)
From Contamines village centre take the road to the Hameau du Lay and park at the chairlift de Montjoie. Walk up to the top of the Hameau du Baptieu. Follow the road (snowed over) which goes up to the Chalets de Colombaz" (1500 m). Climb the pretty, wooded slopes to the right (N.E), pass under the high tension cables and, at around 1850 m, you will find yourself at the base of a shoulder bordered on the right by an outcrop of black schist. Follow this shoulder on the left to its summit, marked 2101 m. Climb again to the left to the col at 2411 m, then once more left to the Tête de la Combaz by the snowy ridge (very close).

- Descent: Same way down.

- Variation
It is generally possible to reach the summit of the Mont Joly on foot.

→

Photo 5:
8. Tête de la Combaz
8a. Mont Joly - variant

9 - THE TRE-LA-TETE HUT (1970m) (access)

- Map : IGN TOP 25 3531 ET St Gervais
- Access : Les Contamines
- Starting point : a) Le Cugnon, b) Notre Dame de la Gorge
- Height difference : 750 m
- Orientation : a) west, b) north then west
- Difficulty : 1)E-IMS, 2) SD-GS
- Timing : 2 - 3hrs
- Time of year : March-June.

- Itineraries (photo 9)

a) Park at the Hameau du Cugnon and follow the path which climbs more or less up the side towards the refuge. This route is very exposed to avalanches in winter when there is a lot of snow, and in spring when the slopes of the Pointe de Chaborgne have not been purged. Avoid the path "variant Bernard" which is very avalanche prone.

b) From Notre Dame de la Gorge climb up the Voie Romaine to the stone bridge, turn left, pass the Chalet de la Laya, cross the bridge of the Combe Noir. Climb the Combe Noir as best you can by the summer path. When you reach a point directly above the "Combe Noire" chalets you can see the summit of the "Tête Noir" and the top of the cable car (EDF). Go up towards these and then traverse across to the hut (1970 m). Can be difficult in places if there is still snow on the path, but it is a better route than the first one.

- Variation

You can reach route b by the lifts and the Col de la Fenetre (see tour n° 1). By this way you can do some downhill skiing.

- Safety Tips:

The first route is easier and more frequently used but is dangerous if there is still snow, especially under the "Pointe du Chaborgne". Do not go, except very early in the morning if it has been well frozen the night before!

10 - LE PAIN DE SUCRE DU MONT TONDU (3169m)
(return trip)

A classic tour from the refuge Tre-la-Tête, with a fabulous view of the glacier and the Italian side of the Mont Blanc.

- Map : IGN TOP 25 3531 ET St Gervais
- Access : Les Contamines
- Starting point : Refuge Tre-la-tête
- Height difference : 1200 m up and down
- Orientation : north-west
- Difficulty : SD+-GS-A
- Timing : 4-5hrs up, 2-2hrs30 down
- Time of year : March-May
- Equipment : as for tours on glaciers.

Itinerary (photo 8)
Follow tour n° 15 to the higher bowl of the Tre-la-Tête Glacier, continue up till you find the bottom of the Mont Tondu glacier. Go up the right bank. Keep the Col du Mont Tondu on your left and traverse up to the right to gain access to the north-west ridge of the Pain du Sucre, continue to the summit.

Descent
Same way down, but it is possible to ski directly down the North face (50m at 40°), before rejoining the route up.

Note: This route is also accessible from the Conscrits Hut.

Variation
You can ski down the left bank of the Mont Tondu glacier if there is good snow cover on the steep (40°) bottom section. Have a look on the way up.

Photo 6: 7a. Descent variant of the Pointe Sud des Monts Jovets
11a. Descent variant of Col des Chasseurs

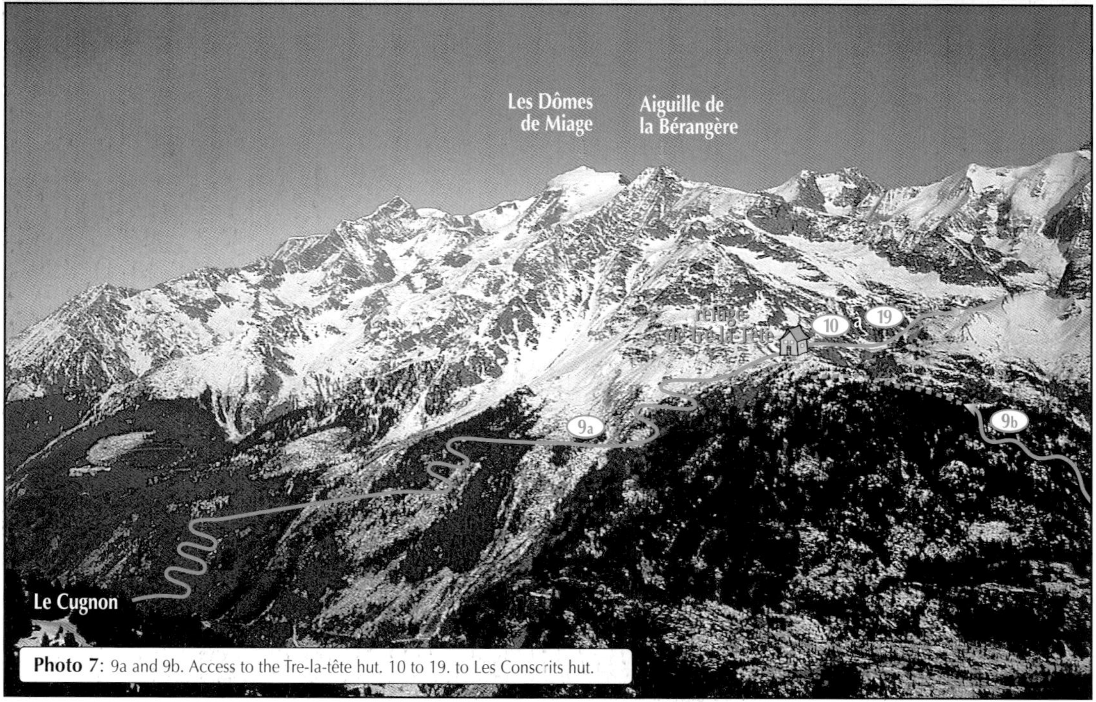
Les Dômes de Miage
Aiguille de la Bérangère
refuge de Tré-la-Tête
10
a
19
9a
9b
Le Cugnon

Photo 7: 9a and 9b. Access to the Tre-la-tête hut. 10 to 19. to Les Conscrits hut.

From the summit it is also possible to descend the south-west side by a complex itinerary which brings you back to the "Jovet" lakes (VGS). Go back down the ridge to the small col between the Pyramide Chaplan and the Pain de Sucre, drop down the west side and descend slightly right on sustained slopes. Come back under the Mont Tondu, then down to the Jovet lakes to rejoin tour n° 7. (photo 4)

- Safety tips
The descent shown on the map TOP 25 to the Jovet lakes is avalanche prone in its bottom part, avoid it!

→

Photo 8:
10. pain de Sucre du Mont Tondu
10a. Descent variant
11. col des Chasseurs - 11a. Descent variant
13c. To Robert Blanc Hut

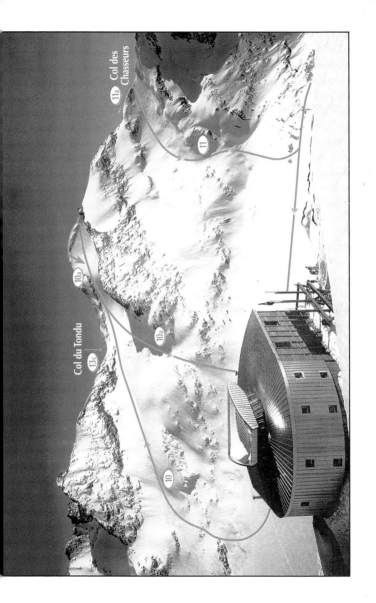

11 - LE COL DES CHASSEURS (2720 m) from the Tré-la-Tête Hut
(return trip)

Similar to the precedent, but shorter and less used. Ideal as a first route before going to the Conscrits refuge.

- Map : IGN TOP 25 3531 ET St Gervais
- Access : Les Contamines
- Starting point : Refuge de Tre-la tête
- Height difference : 750 m up and down
- Orientation : north-east
- Difficulty : SD-GS-A
- Timing : 2hrs30-3hrs up, 1-1hr30 down
- Time of year : March-May
- Equipment : As for tours on glaciers.

- **Itinerary** (photo 8)
  Follow route N° 15 to the upper part of the Tre-la-Tête glacier. Traverse completely over to the left bank of the glacier. Above you a bowl, fairly obvious, takes you to the Col des Chasseurs, which is on the north-east ridge of the Mont Tondu between the Pyramide Chaplan (3035 m) and the Pointe de la Palissade (2720 m).

- **Descent**: Same way down.

- **Variation** (photo 6)
  From the col you can ski down the north-west side into the Combe Blanche by a 40° gully which brings you out onto huge slopes. Climb left up the ridge, then cross up to the right to find the entrance to the gully. From the Combe Blanche see Variant Tour n° 7.

- **Note:** this tour can also be done from the Conscrits hut.

12 - LE COL DES GLACIERS (3063 m)
(return trip)

An obvious col opposite the Conscrits hut, lovely sustained slopes with a passage towards the "Vallee des Chapieu" and the "Robert Blanc" refuge.

- Map	: IGN TOP 25 3531 ET St Gervais
- Access	: Les Contamines
- Starting point	: Refuge Tre-la-Tête
- Height difference	: 1100 m both ways
- Orientation	: north-west
- Difficulty	: SD+GS-A
- Timing	: 4 - 5hrs up, 2 - 3hrs down
- Time of year	: March-May
- Equipment	: as for tours on glaciers

- **Itinerary** (photo 9)
  As for n° 15 to the higher bowl of the Tré-la-Tête glacier. Climb up the bowl to 2500 m where the glacier forms an elbow on the left. Traverse on the right to reach the glacial slope dominated by the Col des Glaciers. Pass either to the right or the left (less steep), of the rocky island rising out of the base of the slope. Climb these north-west slopes towards the col situated near the north buttresses of the Pointe des Lanchettes.

- **Descent**: Same way down (sustained 35° slopes).

- **Variation** (photo 13)
  You can, from the pass, follow the easy rocky ridge to the Col du Moyen Age, then the snowy summit ridge as far as the Dome de Neige des Glaciers (D, there are sometimes big cornices). Come down the same way or follow Tour n° 14.

- **Safety tip**
  Watch out for windslab.

Photo 9: 12. Col des Glaciers
12a. To the col des Glaciers (variant)
13a. and 13c. To the Robert Blanc Hut

to the
Conscrits hutte

Photo 10: 15. Conscrits hut
18. Aiguille de la Bérangère- 18a. descent (variant)
16, 17, 19. to the Col Infranchissable, les Dômes de Miage, L'Aiguille Nord de Tré-la-Tête

13 - THE ROBERT BLANC HUT
(hut access)

A small winter refuge of rare comfort, in a valley generally deserted when the road is snowed over, in which case the access from the Tre-la-Tête bowl is the best solution.

- Map	: IGN TOP 25 3531 ET St Gervais
- Access	: a) Les Contamines, b) Bourg St Maurice
- Starting point	: a) refuge Tre-la-Tête, b) From the Chapieux and the Vallée des Glaciers
- Height difference	: a) 1350 m up, 550 m down. b) 1200 m
- Orientation	: 1) north-west then south, 2) south-west then south
- Difficulty	: a) SD-GS-A, b) E-IMS
- Timing	: a) 3-4hrs up, 1hr30-2hrs down. b) Varies greatly according to snow conditions, perhaps 3hrs from the Chalet des Mottets and 2hrs extra from the Chapieux
- Time of year	: a) March-June; b) June, after the road is cleared
- Equipment	: as for tours on glaciers.

- **Itineraries:** (photo 9 et 13)
   a) From the Tre-la-Tête hut, as for tour n°12 to the Col des Glaciers. Descend the 40°, exposed south side staying well to the left. Cross the rocky outcrop (perhaps an abseil). Depending on conditions, you can also come off the col using a steep couloir (50 m at 45°, fixed rope useful). Descend the little valley bordered on the left by a moraine. Go to the foot of the south ridge of the Pointe des Lanchettes under the point marked 2562 m, go around it and climb up to the right towards the refuge.
   b) From Bourg St Maurice find and park in the Chapieux village (road not cleared in winter). Follow the road above the Chalets des Mottets and continue to the Chalets des Lanchettes. On the left a large valley opens up (facing south-east). Go up the right bank and near 2050 m traverse to the right and continue up (nice slopes!). Leave, again by the right at 2500 m, to climb the indistinct shoulder (steep at first) which brings you to the hut.

- Variation

You can also get to the hut from the Elisabetta hut in Italy (routes n° 68 and n°69) or from Les Contamines and the Col des Fours (routes n°5 and n°6) from where you descend the sustained north-east slopes which bring you, after a little jiggling between the rocks at the bottom of the vallon des tufs, to the "Ville des Glaciers" where you rejoin the way up b.

- Safety tips

The way up a) is reserved for good ski mountaineers, the south slopes must be negotiated early! and a short rope or an abseil are often necessary for access.

The way up b) is easy but very long when the road is closed. This valley is also very avalanche prone.

Note: There are many escape routes from the refuge Robert Blanc.

By the Col du Tondu, (corniced rock outcrop equipped with cables on the south-east side) or by the Col des Glaciers (steep slopes, rocks) to get onto the Glacier de Tre-la-tête.

By the Col de la Seigne to get to the "Val Veny" in Italy, (see tours n° 65 and n° 69).

By the Col de Bonhomme and the Col des Fours, (see tours n° 5 and n° 6) to get back to Les Contamines.

Photo 11: 16,17,19. Col Infranchissable, Dôme de Miage, Aig. Nord de Tré-la-Tête
17a. "Divine Moquette"
17bis a. down to the Glacier d'Armancette - 17bis b. Col De La Bérangère. Direct access.
18. Aiguille de la Bérangère. - 18a and 18b. Descents variants

Aiguille Nord de Tré-la-Tête

to the Col Infranchissable
16

19

to the Conscrits hut

Photo 12: 16. col infranchissable- 19. Aiguille Nord de Tré-la-Tête

14 - DOME DE L'AIGUILLE DES GLACIERS (3592m)
(return trip)

Grand glacial route on sustained, regular slopes, ideal on spring snow, little traffic even in full season.

- Map   : IGN TOP 25 3531 ET St Gervais
- Access   : Les Contamines or Bourg St Maurice
- Starting point : Refuge Robert Blanc
- Height difference : 1100 m up, more than 2000 m down to the Chapieux
- Orientation   : south-west
- Difficulty   : SD-GS-A
- Timing   : 4-5hrs up, 2-3hrs down
- Time of year   : March-June
- Equipment   : as for tours on glaciers.

- **Itinerary** (photo 13)
  From the hut go back down to 2500 m to go around the south ridge of the Pointe des Lanchettes, then climb up the steep slopes bordered on the right by a moraine. Go up the "glacier des Glaciers" keeping to the right bank. At 3200 m approx, come back slightly right under the buttresses of L'Aiguille des Glaciers and climb the steepish slopes onto the Dome de Neige. You can in fact climb easily on skis to the foot of the "L'Aiguille des Glaciers" (3700 m).

- **Descent**: same route down

- **Variation**
  Go down the left bank of the "glacier des Glaciers" towards Les Cabottes, (superb steep slopes, 1000 m at 30°, VGS-A) which take you straight back to the Chalet des Lanchettes.

- **Safety tips:**
  All the way up, look out for the different ways down, especially the bottom part of the "Cabottes" (snow cover, rocks, gullies etc...).

→

Photo 13: Access to the Robert Blanc hut - 12a, 14. Dôme de Neige des Glaciers 14a. The Cabottes descent - variation - 68. Dôme de Neige de l'Aiguille des Glaciers

15 - THE CONSCRITS HUT (2600m)
(hut access)

A new refuge, the old one, nicknamed "Station Mir", was destroyed in the autumn of 1996.

- Map   : IGN TOP 25 3531 ET St Gervais
- Access   : Les Contamines
- Starting point : Refuge des Conscrits (2600 m)
- Height difference : 650 m
- Orientation   : west then south
- Difficulty   : SD-GS-A
- Timing   : 2hrs30-3hrs
- Time of year   : March-June
- Equipment   : as for tours on glaciers.

- Itinerary (photo 10)

Climb up above the Tre-la-Tête hut and traverse to join the foot of a short steep slope. Go up it and leave by the right. Continue traversing until you reach a shelf (cairn). You will find yourselves above a deep, narrow gorge. Descend a little and pass along the foot of a dark rock barrier, often damp (this passage, le Mauvais Pas, is tricky and exposed, you must not fall here). After this traverse, you can either:

-1) By a short descent, rejoin the base of the Tre-la-Tête Glacier.
-2) Follow the summer path which passes sideways on rock slabs, directly onto the glacier.

Go up the centre of the glacier until you reach the Tré-la-Grande seracs. Pass these on the left, next to the cliffs, and climb into the higher bowl of the Tré-la-Tête Glacier. On the right bank of this glacier is an immense jumble of boulders stretching for several kilometres. Go around it to the right, then up alongside for 700 m (approx). Cross through the rocks to find yourself on the steep slopes directly underneath the new hut. Get up as best you can (tricky if the snow is hard).

- Safety Tips

"Le Mauvais Pas" (the bad step) is, like its name suggests, difficult to cross, particularly in winter. The path snakes between a rock barrier and smooth slabs above a boiling, closed in canyon. If the snow is hard you cross on foot, roped up, with crampons. It is subject to avalanches and falling ice after even short periods of rewarming. On returning from the routes in the Tré-la-Tête bowl it is advised to cross before midday.

The new hut is situated below the old one on the summer path and is not on maps printed before 1998.

16 - THE COL INFRANCHISSABLE (3349 m)
(return trip)

The easiest route in this section. Fantastic view over the Italien side of Mont Blanc.

- Map : IGN TOP 25 3531 ET St Gervais
- Access : Les Contamines
- Starting point : Refuge des Conscrits
- Height difference : 770 m up and down
- Orientation : south-west
- Difficulty : E-IMS-A
- Timing : 2hrs30 - 3hrs up, 45 mn down
- Time of year : March-June
- Equipment : as for tours on glaciers.

- **Itinerary** (photos 10 and 11, 12)
  Climb up 100 m above the hut, attack the long ascending traverse (tricky and exposed on hard snow) towards the Tre-la-Tête Glacier, to pass under the base of the south ridge of the Pointe des Conscrits. When you reach the glacier continue up and across till you come directly under the point marked 3169 m (bottom of the south, south-east ridge of the 3633 m Dome). Go on up, avoiding the crevasses by the right, then continue up the centre of the glacier to the col.

- **Descent**: Same way down.

17 - THE DOMES DE MIAGE (3633 m)
(return trip)

//The wind whistles across the passes of the Domes".

- Map   : IGN TOP 25 3531 ET St Gervais
- Access   : Les Contamines
- Starting point   : Refuge des Conscrits
- Height difference : 1050 m up and down
- Orientation   : south-east
- Difficulty   : E-GS-A
- Timing   : 3-4hrs up, 1-2hrs down
- Time of year   : March-June
- Equipment   : as for tours on glaciers.
- Snowboard

- **Itinerary** (photos 10 and 11)
  Climb up 100 m above the hut, attack the long ascending traverse (tricky and exposed on hard snow) towards the Tre-la-Tête Glacier, to pass under the base of the south ridge of the Pointe des Conscrits. When you reach the glacier continue up and across until directly under the point marked 3169 m, (bottom of the south, south-east ridge of the 3633 m Dome). Continue, avoiding the crevasses on their right, then come back left towards the point marked 3336 m. Go up the small valley which takes you to the Col des Domes. From here climb (generally on foot) the steep ridge to the left which rises up to the summit.

- **Descent**
  By the way up. You can descend the south face of the Dome staying close to its south-east ridge, to rejoin the route near the point marked 3169 m. This splendid variation is called Divine Moquette (Divine Carpet).

- **Variation**: by the Glacier d'Armancette (see n°17 bis).

17 BIS - THE GLACIER D'ARMANCETTE
(descent)

A constant steep slope of 2400 m. The Glacier d'Armancette is one of the most formidable in these mountains.

- Height difference : 2400 m down
- Orientation   : down, west then north-west then west
- Difficulty   : SD-VGS-A
- Timing   : 3 - 5hrs down
- Time of year   : March-June
- Equipment   : as for tours on glaciers.

- **Access** (photo 11)
  a) From the Dome, go down to the next small col and climb up on foot (rope, crampons) to the famous exposed ridge which takes you up to the last Dome (3670 m). From the top, go down the west face a few dozen metres then to the left towards the ridge. Above the Col de la Berangere descend a steep slope (150 m at 40°).
  b) It is also possible to access directly the Col de la Berangere. From the Tré-la Tête Glacier go to the foot of the Col de Berangere and climb up on foot the very steep couloir on the right, which comes out just above the col.

- **Descent** (photo 14)
  From the col ski the Armancette Glacier staying mainly right. Near 3100 m go around the left of the serac barrier and back underneath it. Continue down the right bank of the glacier following the rock promontory. Around 2750 m leave the glacier to the right by a short climb to a small col at 2772 m. Ski a large bowl, bordered on the right by a rocky ridge, which finishes with a steep, exposed couloir at 2450 m (50 m at 40°). From the flat area at the bottom, cross to the left to avoid the rock barrier and descend under the point marked 2330 m. Come back to the right in the valley of Covagnet. At the bottom this shrinks and turns into a woody ramp (careful of the rocks to the left,

→

Photo 14:
17 bis. Descent of the Glacier d'Armancette

stay right). This brings you to the "Lac d'Armancette". There you can either take the forest path to the Chalets d'Armancette then the Hameau de la Frasse or, if their is no snow on the last part, descend more to the left by the small paths which arrive at the Cugnon parking.

- **Safety tips**

This descent must be completed early as the Covagnet slopes are fairly avalanche prone in spring. Rope work could be useful at several points. Do not miss the short climb to the right at 2750 m, there is no other way out further down. Attention! this route differs in several places to that marked on the IGN map.

-The marks on the map cross higher up (2850 m - 2900 m) to join the steep avalanche prone slopes which dominate the Pointe de Covagnet. We think the small col at 2772 m is preferable.

-After the steep couloir at 2400 m, the map route goes right onto the rocks, we prefer to cross completely to the left to find less dangerous slopes.

Given the complexity of this descent, only undertake it in excellent visibility.

18 - AIGUILLE DE LA BERANGERE (3425 m)
(return trip)

A short route with a direct access from the hut.

- Map   : IGN TOP 25 3531 ET St Gervais
- Access   : Les Contamines
- Starting point   : Conscrits hut
- Height difference   : 825 m
- Orientation   : south
- Difficulty   : SD+-GS-A
- Timing   : 3hrs up, 1hr down
- Time of year   : March-June
- Equipment   : as for tours on glaciers.

- **Itinerary** (photos 10 and 11)
Go straight up above the refuge, towards the north-east, by steep slopes. Then near 3000 m, turn slightly to the right. At 3200 m you arrive at a snowy cirque bordered on the right by a ridge overlooking the Tre-la-Tête Glacier. Go up the right side of the following slope, then left to the rocky base of the Aiguille de la Berangere. Climb the last slope on foot by either the obvious snow gully to the right, or the ridge to the left.

- **Descent**: same way down.

- **Variation**
To avoid repassing the refuge, (the descent underneath is not easy) go leftwards to a small col between the "Aiguille de la Bérangère" and the "Pointe des Conscrits" (at approx. 3260 m). You can descend either to the left by a steep passage (often corniced), or by carrying straight on down. In both cases go back to the right bank of the "Tré-la-Tête" glacier.

19 - AIGUILLE DE TRE-LA-TETE - The north summit
(return)

A magnificent ski mountaineering route, rarely done, on a bleak and steep north-west face.

- Map   : IGN TOP 25 3531 ET St Gervais
- Access   : Les Contamines
- Starting point : Conscrits hut
- Height difference : 1290 m
- Orientation   : north-west
- Difficulty   : VD-VGS-A
- Timing   : 4-5hrs up, 1-2hrs down
- Time of year   : March-June
- Equipment   : as for tours on glaciers.

- **Itinerary** (photos 10, 11 and 12)
  From 100 m above the hut make a long climbing traverse in the direction of the Glacier de Tré-La-Tête (difficult and exposed on hard snow), to pass under the base of the south ridge of the Pointe des Conscrits and climb until directly under the point marked 3169 m (the bottom of the south, south-east ridge of the 3633 m sumit). Traverse right, direction Col Infranchissable, reach the glacier of the north-west face of the Aiguille Nord by the left (under the Tête Carrée). Cross on foot the first bergschrund on its left then come back to the right to reach less steep slopes.
  Around 3750 m cross another bergschrund, and climb up (on foot) the steep slope which takes you onto the ridge. Follow it to the top.

- **Descent**: By the same route.
  We would generally leave our skis under the second bergschrund.
  (the final slope is steep, 45°, often icy and exposed)

Variation

From the top it is possible to reach the Lex Blanche glacier on the Italian side. Follow the ridge in the direction of the Aiguille Centrale, then descend several metres to a small col. On your right a steep couloir (100 m at 40°) brings you onto the suspended glacier of the west face of the Aiguille Nord. Cross this glacier horizontally to the base of the promontory coming off of the Aiguille Centrale. Descend an exposed slope (25 m at 40°, fixed rope useful) working left to a flat spot. From there a new wall (150 m at 40°) with sometimes a large bergschrund brings you onto the Glacier Lex Blanche. The route down to the Elisabetta hut (Val Veny, tour n° 67) is long and peppered with crevasses, but what a ride!

20 - LE MONTHIEU (2302 m)
(return trip)

The perfect pyramid which dominates the Contamines.

- Map : IGN TOP 25 3531 ET St Gervais
- Access : Les Contamines
- Starting point : Hameau de la Frasse (1263 m)
- Height difference : 1050 m
- Orientation : south-west
- Difficulty : SD-VGS
- Timing : 3 - 4 hrs up, 1 - 2 hrs down
- Time of year : December-April.

- **Itinerary**
From the Hameau de la Frasse take the forest trail south and then a path through the forest to the Lac d'Armancette, go diagonally left and traverse across the huge slopes of the Monthieu which you climb near to the north-west ridge.

- **Descent:** by the same route.

- **Safety Tips**
Lovely ski down, but prone to avalanches and wind slab. Only go in good conditions.

→
Photo 15:
20. Le Monthieu

Le Monthieu

20

21 - LE COL DE TRICOT (2120 m)
(return trip)

A little known route with a magnificent view of the north face of the Aiguille de Bionnassay.

- Map   : IGN TOP 25 3531 ET St Gervais
- Access   : Les Contamines
- Starting point : Le Champel
- Height difference : 720 m
- Orientation   : west then north
- Difficulty   : E+-GS.
- Timing   : 3-3hrs30 up, 1-3hrs down.
- Time of year   : December-March.

- **Itinerary** (photos 16 and 17)
  From Bionnay either walk or drive (depending on conditions) to the "Hameau de Champel". Go through the village and follow a forest trail to the "Chalet du Chalère". Go up to the right on the steeper wooded slopes. A narrow steep passage allows you to climb above the rock barrier and brings you onto the left bank of the "Bionnassay Glacier". Follow the moraines of the left bank then after crossing diagonally right, come down a few metres to a flat area, then climb the obvious bowl to the "Col de Tricot".

- **Descent**: Same way down.

- **Variations**
  It is possible to leave the village of "Bionnassay" following tour n° 22.
  -Tour du Mont Vorassay.
  From the col descend the south face on the 30° slopes which bring you to the "Chalets de Miage". Cross the stream, and after a short climb, follow the forest trail to the right as far as the "Maison Neuve". Continue the descent to the "Hameau de la Gruvaz". Take the road down to the main St Gervais-Les Contamines road, then back to Bionnay (2.5 kms). This can only be done in very good conditions because the south face is avalanche prone and the snow doesn't last long.

→

Photo 16: 21. col du Tricot

Mont Vorassay

Col
de Tricot

21

22 - THE REFUGE DE TETE ROUSSE (3162 m)
(hut access)

An exceptional route, rarely used, on the snow fields dominating the Glacier de Bionnassay.

- Map   : IGN TOP 25 3531 ET St Gervais
- Starting point   : Bionnassay
- Height difference   : 1760 m
- Orientation   : west
- Difficulty   : D-VGS-A
- Timing   : 6-7 hrs up, 2-3 hrs down
- Time of year   : February-April
- Equipment   : as for tours on glaciers.

- Itinerary (photo 17)
Park at the "Hameau de Crozat" and follow the forest trail east (electric pylons). At roughly 1610 m cross a bottleneck to the right (tricky) and enter the forest. As best you can follow the summer path to the footbridge (dismantled in winter). Swim the stream naked, to keep your clothes dry (only joking), and climb the steep, narrow slope opposite which brings you onto the glacier. Climb up the left bank to the serac barrier which you climb by a steep slope. Take this passage to the foot of the rock buttresses of the "Tricot" ridge. At 2170 m traverse the vast flat area to the left to reach the right side of the glacier. Climb up a very steep slope (Desert de Pierre Ronde), then climb the succession of small valleys next to the glacier. Around 2600 m go back onto the glacier and climb up to the point marked 2959 m. Leave the glacier and follow a steep bowl to the left to reach the refuge.

- Descent:
-same way down.
-or by a couloir (200m at 35-40°) down to the "Tête Rousse Glacier". From the refuge descend right, then plunge left of the point marked 3132 m. At the bottom, rejoin the route by going left.

- **Safety tips**: it is tempting to go up to the refuge by following the Mont Blanc Tramway. Although a lot shorter from the top of the Les Houches lifts, the rails go through two tunnels which are blocked off when the railway line is not in use. It is extremely dangerous to try to go around them!

23 - LE MONT BLANC (4807 m)

(traverse)

An original route, completely deserted at this time of year.

- Map : IGN TOP 25 3531 ET St Gervais
- Starting point : Bionnassay
- Height difference : 1st day 1750m, 2nd day 650 m, 3rd day 1000 m
- Orientation : West then North-West
- Difficulty : VD-VGS-A
- Timing : 1st day 6-7hrs up, 2nd day 3-3hrs30 up,
  3rd day 5-7hrs up, 3-6hrs down.
- Time of year : May-June
- Equipment : as for tours on glaciers.

- **Itinerary** (photos 17, 18 and 19)

-**Day 1**). Depending on the snow, either:

1). From the "Crozat"car park , follow the "Chalet de L'Are" path. Pass just under the chalet taking the path which climbs up the moraine on the right bank of the "Bionnassay" glacier. At 2000 m there is a rock barrier, from here the route becomes very steep with exposed parts (ladders only in summer). It snakes across some slabs before rejoining tour n° 22 around 2200 m.

2). Follow tour n° 22 to the "Tête Rousse" refuge.

- **Day 2**). From the refuge, go up the first slopes towards the west face of the "Aiguille du Gouter". Above the point marked 3270 m, cross a snow couloir to the right (cables) to arrive at the bottom of a rock promontory (not very distinct). Climb up a few metres to come in line with the centre of this promontory. Follow it up staying on the ridge as much as possible (red marked path). From time to time cables are in place to help you up the steeper parts (easy climbing).

Photo 17: 21. Col de Tricot - 22. Climb to the "refuge de Tête Rousse"
22a. Descent variant - 23. Climb to the "refuge du Goûter"

- **Day 3)**. Go up a few metres above the refuge and follow the ridge to the right. A short descent brings you to the foot of the north-west face of the "Dome du Gouter". Climb it, going around the seracs either right or left. Around 4250 m traverse left to get over a snowy shoulder and pass onto the north-east side of the "Dome du Gouter". Reach the "Col du Dome" by traversing slightly down (The top of tour n° 24 "The Grand Mulets"). From here you climb a steep bump, often icy, which brings you to a refuge/bivouac (the Vallot hut) situated to the left, just under the observatory (closed to the public). On foot follow the "Bosses" ridge to the summit.

- **Descent** (photo 18)

  Go back down past the Vallot hut to the "Col du Dome", then right to the "Grand Plateau". Go to the left and weave between the seracs and crevasses to the "Petit Plateau". Descend the"Petites Montées" staying on the right, then crab left to the "Ilots Rocheux" (rocky islands 3330 m). Go to the right, taking a long traverse to arrive under the "Grands Mulets" refuge (on a rock spur). The itinerary between the "Grand Plateau" and the "Grands Mulets" varies every year, glaciers move constantly and snow cover must be considered. From the "Grands Mulets" ski over to the "Plan de L'Aiguille" then down to Chamonix (tour n° 24).

- **Variation**

  The descent of the north face. Steep and complex route at the bottom, abseils (see tour n° 24).

  Descent by the "Passage du Corridor" (Tour 25)

- **Safety tips**: the Mont Blanc by the Gouter refuge is a hefty enterprise on skis. The routes presented are the only ones recommended. It would be extremely dangerous to try to follow the tramway lines if they were under snow. But at the beginning of certain summers, with good late snow, it is possible to do it from the "Nid d'Aigle" when the tramway opens. But don't expect solitude, beware of falling rocks, especially on the Gouter face, and wear a hard hat.

CHAMONIX
MONT-BLANC

Le Mont Blanc, highest point in Europe, is a true magnet which attracts people from all over the world. At 4807 m it dominates the valley of Chamonix, visible from the town and one of the biggest skiable height differences in the world. Some years you can put your skis on at the top and take them off in town. The worst part is that its slopes are sometimes covered with people in the spring, the refuges at bursting point, long queues at the Midi lift station, the price of glory! The Vallée Blanche is now a great classic, more an off-piste descent than a tour. Some of the other valleys of the region, like the Glacier du Mont Mallet or the Cirque de Talefre, have stayed surprisingly wild, especially in winter and spring. The setting is particularly impressive between the Grands Jorasses, the Aiguille Verte and the high wall complexes of the Aiguilles de Chamonix.

Access

By car: Motorway from Lyon and Geneva, national roads from Albertville, Megeve and St Gervais. From Italy, by the Mont Blanc Tunnel, (when and if it re-opens in the fall of the year 2000).
From Switzerland, by Martigny and the Col de la Forclaz.
By Train: SNCF station Chamonix, from Switzerland by Martigny.

Lodgings

No shortage here, hotels, rented flats etc., but reservations are often necessary well in advance. There are also several "Gites" (dormitories), usually out of the centre.
- Gite La Montagne, (Bouchet): 04 50 53 11 60.
- Gite Le Chamoniard Volant, (La Frasse): 04 50 53 14 09.
- Gite La Tapia: 04 50 53 18 19.
- Gite La Bagna, (Les Praz): 04 50 53 62 90.
Kosciusko Lodge: 04 50 53 38 09.
For more information, Chamonix Tourist office: 04 50 53 00 24.
Les Houches: 04 50 55 50 62. St Gervais: 04 50 47 76 08.

Refuges

Tête Rousse, (3162m) CAF, 57 places, always open, unmanned in spring, Tel: 04 50 58 24 97.
Gouter, (3817m) CAF, 120 places, always open, unmanned in spring, Tel: 04 50 54 40 93.
Grands Mulets, (3051m) CAF, 68 places, always open, manned from March- September, Tel: 04 50 53 16 98.
Cosmiques, (3613m) private, manned from February-October, Tel: 04 50 54 40 16. The Abri Simond hut serves in winter, 100 m above the refuge at the foot of the Cosmiques ridge.
Vallot, (4362m) always open, for emergencies only.
Requin, CAF, 74 places, always open, manned winter and spring, Tel: 04 50 53 16 96.
Leschaux, CAF, 16 places, always open, unmanned in spring.
Couvercle, CAF, 120 places, manned in spring, Tel: 04 50 53 16 94.
Winter hut, 30 places, situated under the huge rock slab.

Useful addresses
- Chamonix tourist office: 04 50 53 00 24. Reservations desk: 04 50 53 23 33. minitel: 3615 Chamonix.
- Association International des Guides du Mont Blanc: 04 50 53 27 05.
- Compagnie des Guides de Chamonix : 04 50 53 00 88.
- Office de la Haute Montagne: 04 50 53 22 08., for information on routes and conditions.
- P.G.H.M: 04 50 53 16 89, Police, Mountain Rescue.
- Train Station: 04 50 53 00 44, SNCF timetables: 08 36 35 35 35.
- Taxi :04 50 93 61 47.
- Bus SAT: 04 50 78 05 33.
- Aiguille du Midi cable car: 04 50 53 30 80.
- Montenvers Tramway: 04 50 53 12 54.
- Ski rental: Snell sports: 04 50 53 02 17.

Ski lifts
- Aiguille du Midi: Open all year, a lot of ski tours are made easy by the presence of this cable car, which gives rapid access to the high mountains and notably the Vallée Blanche, with its enormous possibilities for off piste and steeps.
- Montenvers: Open all year, the "Cremaillere" (Cog railway) the most famous in the world, is often used as the quick way down at the end of the season when the path down to Chamonix is not possible on skis. The way to the station from the Mer de Glace is as follows.
  1) By the cable car "Grotte de Glace", a short icy passage to the bottom station.
  2) Above the train station look out for a huge white square, get up as best you can using a system of ladders which take you up to the path to the station.
- Lift passes: There is the Chamski pass which gives access to all the lifts and buses in the valley, daypasses and single tickets are also available.
- Buses: centralised system which gives access to most of the valley.
- Trains: Run the length of the valley, giving access to all districts.

Starting points for the tours:
- the Aiguille de Midi cable car, at the entrance to Chamonix South, follow the signs for the carpark.
- Montenvers Train, at the entrance to Chamonix, parking on the left after the level crossing.

24 - LE MONT BLANC
by the refuge Grands Mulets (3051m)
(return trip)

The classic route for the Mont Blanc on skis.

- Map : IGN TOP 25 3531 ET St Gervais
- Starting point : Midi cable car
- Height difference : Day 1: 825 m; Day 2: 1750 m
- Orientation : Day 1: north-west; Day 2: north
- Difficulty : D-GS-A
- Timing : Day1: 3-4hrs up, Day2: 6-8hrs up, 3-4hrs down
- Time of year : March-June
- Equipment : as for tours on glaciers.

- **Itinerary** (photos 18 and 19)
  - **Day1**: From the "Plan de Midi" (middle station of the cable car), climb up in the direction of the north face of the "Aiguille de Midi" (path sometimes visible) to step onto the glacier "des Pelerins". Traverse it rightwards and climb a short steep slope at around 2500-2550 m. A long traverse right then a descent takes you onto the glacier "des Bossons" above the old cable car station. Cross the glacier at a flat area called the "Plan Glacier" to reach the "Jonction", a crevassed confluence zone. Climb north to the rock promontory of the "Grands Mulets"; the refuge is on its southern tip.
  - **Day2**
    a) *by the classic route*:
    From the refuge, climb the glacier rightwards towards its left bank (point marked 3330 m). Come back to the middle of the glacier and climb up a steep section on the left, (Les Petites Montées). From here you can gain access to the "Petit Plateau". Go up the left side to arrive at the foot of the "Grandes Montées", then, as best you can climb up to the "Grand Plateau". Go up the less sustained slopes to the right which bring you to the "Col des Domes". A short steep slope to the left brings you to the Vallot hut (now in view) at 4363 m. Most of the skiers leave their skis at the hut.

Follow now on foot (rope; crampons; ice-axe) the long and exposed ridge to the top (1hr30 climb).

b) *By the north ridge of the "Dome du Gouter"*
Difficulty: VD-VGS-A.
From the refuge work your way right to the base of the "Arete Nord du Dome" at about 3200 m. Pass under the rocks (point marked 3330 m) and get up as best you can (often on foot near the top) these sustained, crevassed slopes of the north ridge of the Dome. It gets less steep near the "Pointe de Bravais" (4507 m). Go to the "Col de Dome" to rejoin route A.

- Descent: Same way back to the "Plan de L'Aiguille".

- Variation
Down the north face: GS-A.
300 m at 40°.
Without being extreme, this descent demands great prudence. Tiredness and altitude can affect your abilities and judgement! Also the condition of the snow (ice) doesn't always permit this descent. Have a very good look on the way up! Avoid the often icy north summit slope by entering the face at the level of the "Rochers de la Tournette". One or two abseils may be necessary on the bottom part to get back down to the "Grand Plateau".

- Safety tips:
  - Be careful on the short descent to the glacier des Bossons of avalanches, ice and rocks falling off the "glacier Rond".
  - At the same height as the old cable car station, there are two automatic avalanche triggering systems which protect the tunnel.
  - Route a) is the traditional way off the Col de Dome on skis, but is not recommended on the way up as there is too high a risk of falling seracs between 3300 m and 4000 m. This means 2-3hrs exposure to danger.

- Route b) is highly recommended, safer but technically more difficult, it is little used but we hope that it will become the classic.
- The day before you go it would make sense to get to know the first part.

Photo 18:
23. The Mont- Blanc by the Goûter
24. Route to the Grand Mulet
24a. Classic route to Mont-Blanc
24b. Mont Blanc by the north ridge of the Dome
24c. Descent by the north face of Mont-Blanc
25c. "The 3 Mont Blanc"
25a. les corridors

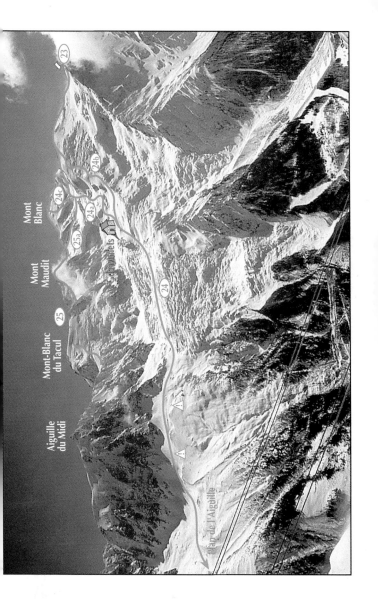

25 - THE THREE MONT-BLANC (4807)
(return trip or circuit)

Long, technical and commiting, in short a ski-mountaineering must. This route is only possible if the snow cover is stabilised. Recommended to snow boarders if it's firm enough to walk up it.

- Map   : IGN TOP 25 3531 ET St Gervais and 3630 OT Chamonix
- Starting-point   : Midi cable car
- Height difference : 1300 m up, 3800 m all the way down to Chamonix!
- Orientation   : north
- Difficulty   : VD-VGS-A
- Timing   : 5-8hrs up, 3-4hrs down
- Time of year   : May to the beginning of July
- Equipment   : as for tours on glacier.
- Snowboard

- **Itinerary** (photos 18 and 19)
  - **Day 1**: from the top station of the Midi cable car, go down the east ridge on foot. Then ski down to the right under the foot of the south face of the "Aiguille de Midi" and the "Cosmiques" ridge. Climb up 50 m to the refuge on the rock shoulder (3613 m).
  - **Day 2**: from the refuge go down and right to the "Col du Midi". Climb up, usually on foot, the north face of the "Mont Blanc du Tacul", to get to the right side of the shoulder of the "Tacul". Make a slight descending traverse towards the "Col Maudit". Cross over to the right under an exposed serac barrier and climb the north face of the "Mont Maudit" to arrive, via very steep slopes, under the "Col du Mont Maudit" to the right of the summit. The col is often barred by a difficult bergschrund. Climb the col by an often icy slope (belays possible on the rock). Traverse left without losing height to

→

Photo 19:
23, 24. Les Bosses ridge
24c. descent of the Mont-Blanc north face
25. Les "Trois Mont-Blanc" - 25b. Mont Blanc du Tacul, variation to the top

Mont-Blanc
du Tacul

25b

Mont
Maudit

Mont-Blanc

25

25

23 24 24c

25

Col du Midi

the "Col de la Brenva" (4303 m). Climb the 40° slope (Mur de la Cote) and the following slopes, passing to the right of the "Petits Rochers Rouge" (4577 m) then to the left of the "Petits Mulets" (4690 m). A last effort on a large regular slope and you're there.

- Descents

By the same way, 40° passages on the "Mur de la Cote" and the north face of the "Mont Maudit" (rope often necessary), 35° passages on the north face of the "Mont Blanc du Tacul". From the "Col du Midi" join the "Valley Blanche", (tour n° 26) if conditions permit. The descent from the summit of Mont Blanc to Chamonix is exceptional and certainly something to remember.

- Variations

- *Descent by the north face*: (see tour n° 24).
- *Descent by the "Corridors" route*: From the "Col de la Brenva" ski down to the north then to the left, alongside the "Rochers Rouge Inferiors", get to the "Grand Plateau" by a 35° crevassed slope, then follow tour n° 24.
- *Climb the "Mont Blanc du Tacul"*: follow the shoulder to the short rock bastion, climb it as best you can, usually on the left.

- Safety tips:

For fit experienced ski mountaineers only, these steep north slopes are avalanche prone, not to be done after a fresh snowfall.

26 - LA VALLEE BLANCHE
(descent)

The grand classic of glacial off piste, certain days a motorway, perfect introduction to glacier skiing and getting to know the Mont Blanc mountains.

- Map   : IGN TOP 3630 OT Chamonix, or 25 3531 ET St Gervais.
- Starting point   : Midi cable car.
- Height difference   : 2000 m to 2800 m down depending of the snow conditions.
- Orientation   : south-east then north.
- Difficulty   : From IMS-A to VGS-A.
- Timing   : 3-5 hrs.
- Time of year   : December- May.
- Equipment   : as for tours on glaciers.

- **Itinerary** (photo 20)
  From the station, walk down the east ridge (fixed ropes in winter) then ski down to the right towards the south face of the Midi and follow the gentle slopes to the " Col du Gros Rognon" (Natural pylon of the Valley Blanche gondola). Continue down the "Glacier du Geant", staying on the shallowest slopes possible (large curve right). Around 3000 m, a long traverse back left brings you to the "Petit Rognon". From here descend as best you can the "seracs du Geant", (crevasses everywhere) and pass underneath the refuge "Requin", (seracs fall frequently, don't hang about). You arrive at a flat area on the right (Salle à Manger). Go to the right, then straight down the middle of the Glacier du Tacul (very flat) to where it joins the glacier de Leschaux (crevasses). Follow the Mer de Glace staying mainly left. Pass under the Montenvers train station, down the last part of the glacier, and leave by the left (1600 m) to make the short climb up right to the "Chalet des Mottets" (drinks and snacks). Then skis back on and down the forest path which snakes down and crosses the railway line. From here continue on to the "Planards" piste and back down to Chamonix.
  In case of a lack of snow take the well visible telecabine from the glacier to the Montenvers train station.

- Variations

There are many possible variations, which generally get harder the further left you go from the normal route. These routes are highly crevassed (see "Chamonix off Piste" by Francois Burnier and Dominique Potard).

- Safety Tips

- Be wary when you cross the serac du Geant area (crevasses and seracs fall).
- Be careful when you arrive at the Planards piste, there are beginners and children.

→

Photo 20:

26. The Valley Blanche route and route to the Requin hut
26a. Petit Envers - 26b. Grand Envers
27. To the col d'Entreves and Pointe Helbronner
27a. To the combe Maudite
61a. to the col de Toule from Aiguille du Midi
62. to the Brenva glacier

Aiguille
du Plan

Aiguille
du Midi

Cosmiques Hut

26b

26a

Requin Hut

Séracs du Géant

26

27a

61a

62

27

to the Mer de Glace

27 - COL D'ENTREVES (3527 m)
(return trip)

S hort introductory tour on skins before continuing down the Valley Blanche.

- Map   : IGN TOP 25 3630 Chamonix
- Starting point   : Midi top station
- Height difference : 330 m up, minimum 2300 m down
- Orientation   : south-east then north
- Difficulty   : E-GS-A
- Timing   : 1 - 1hr30 up, 2 - 4hrs down
- Time of year   : January-May
- Equipment   : as for tours on glaciers.

- **Itinerary** (photos 20 and 21)
  As for n° 26 to the "Col du Gros Rognon", and down the "Glacier du Geant". Around 3200 m, after the "Pointe Adolfe Rey", where the "combe Maudite" joins, put your skins on and climb up towards the "Aiguille de Toule" (crevasses). Then climb the easy valley to the right, between the Tour Ronde" and the "Aiguille d'Entreves" up to the Col.

- **Descent**: by the same route, then as for n° 26, the Valley Blanche.

- **Variation**
  You can also climb the "combe Maudite" to the right, a pretty trip at the foot of the impressive granite faces of the Grand Capucin, the chandle du Tacul etc... Or, from the col, descend the Italian side by the "Glacier d'Entreves", very steep, GS-A, rope obligatory, to the mid station of the "Helbronner" cable car (see tour n° 61).

- **Safety tips:** don't stop to put your skins on between the Pyramide du Tacul and the Pointe Adolfe Rey, very real danger of falling seracs from a suspended glacier, just look up! →

Photo 21:
26. Vallee Blanche
27. Col d'Entreves - 27a. "combe Maudite" - 61a. to "col de Toule" from Aiguille du Midi
62. to the Brenva Glacier - 62c. To the Brenva Glacier by the Tour Ronde

92

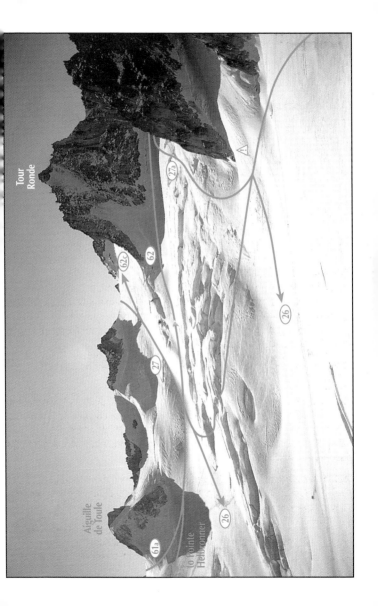

28 - COL DU TACUL (3337m)
(return trip)

Super slopes where you can still find some powder when the Valley Blanche is already skied out.

- Map   : IGN TOP 25 3630 OT Chamonix
- Starting point   : Midi top station
- Height difference : 890 m up, 2900 m down
- Difficulty   : SD-GS-A
- Timing   : 4-4hrs30 up, 2-3hrs down
- Time of year   : January-May
- Equipment   : as for tours on glaciers.

- **Itinerary** (photos 20 and 22)

As for n° 26, the Valley Blanche to the "Salle à Manger" and the right bank of the "Glacier du Tacul". Climb up the right bank of the "Glacier des Periades". At 2800 m, cross up to the left to a large bowl which rises up towards the "col du Tacul". Leave your skis near the bergshrund (3200 m approx.) and climb the right branch of the couloir which goes directly to the pass. You can climb, if you like, the "Aiguille du Tacul" (3444 m) by an easy rock ridge (loose rocks).

- **Descent**

Same way down to 2800 m, then more to the right on steeper, but less crevassed, slopes then wide gullies which bring you back onto the "Glacier du Tacul" and the Valley Blanche (n° 26).

- **Variation**

Descent of the "Petit Capucin" Glacier (VGS-A). From the col, find the belay slings on the north-east side and make a steep abseil for about 50 m. The following 150 m are at 45° or more and you may need to abseil. Then ski down the 35-40° slopes to the Leschaux Glacier, coming off the Capucin glacier by its right bank. Rejoin the Mer de Glace and route n° 26.

29 - BRECHE PUISEUX (3432m)
(circuit)

A pure ski mountaineering traverse with a climb in a steep couloir and then a descent opposite the Grandes Jorasses.

Map	: IGN TOP 25 3630 OT Chamonix
Starting point	: top station of Midi cable car
Height difference	: 1040 m up, 3000m down
Orientation	: north-west, couloir south-west, descent north-east
Difficulty	: D+/VD- GS-A
Timing	: 3hrs30-4hrs30 up, 2-3hrs down
Time of year	: February-May
Equipment	: as for tours on glaciers.

- **Itinerary** (photos 20 and 22)
  As for n° 28, The Col du Tacul, to the point where it branches left, at about 2800 m. Then work east towards the "Pointe Sisyphe".
  Around 3000 m, go right round a rock island and up a steep slope. The south-west couloir is just visible from here to the left. Climb it with your skis on your pack (300 m at 45°) to the "Breche Puiseux". From there a 40 m abseil (equipped with slings on the right) puts you onto the Mont Mallet glacier.

- **Descent** (photo 26)
  Down the highly crevassed Mont Mallet glacier staying mainly to the left. At 2750 m two possibilities open up.
  1) Straight down the left side where, depending on the snow cover, you could find icy patches and rocks appearing.
  2) Go way to the right to find less steep slopes.
  Both take you down to the Leschaux Glacier, stay near the middle down to the "Glacier du Tacul" and the Valley Blanche.

- **Variation**
  After the abseil continue to the Mont Mallet bergschrund (see tour n° 32). The descent by the way up is EGS-A in the couloir.

- Safety tips:

Slings, 2x40 m ropes, ice axes and crampons indispensable.
Setting up an abseil necessitates, besides the knowledge of descending and
self assuring techniques, the verification of the state of the anchor.

Photo 22:
28. Col du Tacul
28a. "Col du Tacul" Variation
29. Breche Puiseux

Col du
Tacul

Brèche
Puiseux

28a

28a

28

29

30 - COL DE LA BUCHE (2785m)
(circuit)

Steep slopes, up and down, often with good powder.

- Map   : IGN TOP 25 3630 OT Chamonix
- Starting point   : Plan de l'Aiguille (Mid station of the Midi cable car)
- Height difference   : 475 m up, 1000 minimum down
- Orientation   : North-west then south-west up, east then north down
- Difficulty   : VD-VGS-A
- Timing   : 1hr30-2hrs up, 1-2hrs30 down
- Time of year   : December-April
- Equipment   : as for tours on glaciers.

- **Itinerary** (drawing n° 23)
  From the mid station (2310 m) go slightly down to the left to the "Lac du Plan" (not really visible in winter) and traverse horizontally towards the Aiguille de l'M crossing the "glacier de Blaitière" and several moraines. After the last moraine (obvious) race across the "glacier des Nantillons" (serac fall danger) to arrive at the foot of the south-west couloir of the "Col de la Buche", which you climb up on foot.

- **Descent**:
  By the east couloir, then to the right to the ladders of the path up to the "Envers des Aiguilles" refuge. Go down the ladders or the slopes to the left, back to the Mer de Glace and the bottom of the Valley Blanche, (n° 26).

- **Safety tips**:
  - a large cornice can complicate the start, avoid it on the right.
  - a serious observation of the snow conditions from the "Mer de Glace" is necessary.

→
Draw 23:
Route to the "Col de la Buche" from the Aiguille mid station

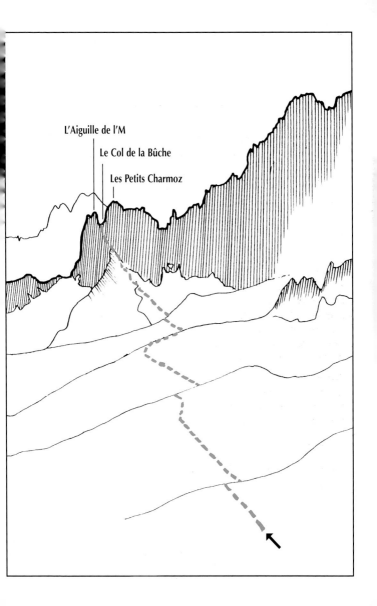

L'Aiguille de l'M

Le Col de la Bûche

Les Petits Charmoz

Col de la Bûche

30

Mer de Glace

Montenvers

26

31 - "REFUGE DE LESCHAUX" (2431m)
(Hut access)

An aluminium box stuck to the rocks, opposite the Jorasses.

- Map   : IGN TOP25 3630 OT Chamonix
- Starting point   : Midi top station
- Height difference : 1600m down, with 330m up
- Difficulty   : E-IMS-A
- Timing   : 1-2hrs up, 1hr30-2hrs30 down
- Time of year   : March-June
- Equipment   : as for tours on glaciers.

- **Itinerary** (photos 20 and 25)
  As for n° 26 The Valley Blanche to the base of the Leschaux glacier at 2100 m.
  Go diagonally to the right as best you can between the rocks and the crevasses and climb up the Leschaux glacier by its right bank. At about 2350 m you should see the refuge on top of a rock barrier. Leave your skis at the bottom of the first couloir to the right of the refuge. Go a little way up before climbing off to the left on easy rock.

- **Variation**
  You can go up to the refuge from Chamonix or from the Montenvers train station (1380 m and 630 m up respectively, 5-7hrs and 3-3hrs30).

- **Safety tips**:
  The last slope up to the refuge can be difficult in bad conditions, don't hesitate to put your crampons on.
  Too many people? The refuge is not very large, better to get there early, eat, and grab a mattress.

←

Photo 24:
30. "Col de la Buche" Descent

32 - MONT MALLET BERGSCHRUND (3700m)
(return)

Excellent glacial route, in one of the furthest corners of these mountains, between the Grandes Jorasses and the Periades.

- Map   : IGN TOP 25 3630 OT Chamonix
- Starting point   : Refuge Des Leschaux
- Height difference : 1300 m
- Orientation   : north-east then north
- Difficulty   : SD-GS-A
- Timing   : 4hr30-5hrs30 up, 1hr30-2hrs30 down
- Time of year   : March-June
- Equipment   : as for tours on glaciers.

- Itinerary (photo 25, 26)
From the refuge go back down onto the Leschaux glacier, then climb up the middle of the Mont Mallet glacier to 2700/2750 m. Take a climbing traverse to the right, keeping well to the right hand side (left bank), until you reach (approx. 3400 m) more gentle slopes. Generally you climb up just to the entrance of the small glacial valley where the route becomes very exposed to serac falls (3700 m).

- Descent
Same way down. From around 2750 m you can continue down the left bank of the Mont Mallet glacier on 35° slopes which arrive back at the Leschaux glacier.

- Variations
- You can get to this route from the "Breche Puiseux" (see tour n° 29).
- There is also the "Col des Grandes Jorasses" (3825 m, E. Canzio bivouac, 10 places). The last slope is 50°, sometimes icy so use crampons.
- For lovers of the steeps, there is the south-west couloir of the "Aiguille de l'Eboulement" (50°, VD-EGS-A) - (photo 26).

→

Photo 25:
29. To the"Breche Puiseux"
32. To Mont Mallet Bergschrund - 32a. To the "Col des Grandes Jorasses" Variations

33 - THE "REFUGE DU COUVERCLE"
(hut access)

A large stone refuge in the middle of the Talefre cirque.

- Map   : IGN TOP 25 3630 OT Chamonix
- Starting point   : Aiguille du Midi top station (or Montenvers top station)
- Height difference : 1700 m down, 600 m back up
- Orientation   : north, then south-west
- Difficulty   : SD- GS-A.
- Timing   : 1hr30-2hrs30 down, 2-3hrs up
- Time of year   : March-June
- Equipment   : as for tours on glaciers.

- **Itinerary** (photos 20, 26 and 27)
  As for tour n° 26, the Valley Blanche, to the base of the Leschaux Glacier at around 2100 m. Get through the rocks and crevasses as best you can, then climb up the right bank of the glacier. At around 2250 m to 2300 m, go up a steep moraine keeping to the left (preferably on foot). 50 m higher you come out onto a large shelf. Go left up steep slopes to an obvious rock landmark, "La Pierre à Beranger". Above this climb a small valley with a moraine on the left. At the top go left to find yourselves on the Talefre glacier. Cross over to the right bank, climb the steep moraine and traverse horizontally to easily reach the refuge.

- **Descent**
  Follow your tracks back.

- **Safety tips**
  The summer path, with its series of ladders, is difficult if there's still snow on it.

→

Photo 26:
29. Breche Puiseux: way back - 31. Leschaux hut - 32. to the Mallet bergschund
32b. To the "Aiguille de l'Eboulement" south-west couloir - 33. "Refuge Couvercle"

Aiguille
de l'Eboulement

refuge de Leschaux

Montenvers
Mer de Glace

34 - THE WHYMPER COULOIR BERGSCHRUND (around 3400 m)
(return trip)

The Whymper couloir is the normal route to the Aiguille Verte. To reach its bergschund is the easiest route in this section.
Short, little frequented, something to fall back on in mediocre weather.

- Map   : IGN TOP 25 3630 OT Chamonix
- Starting point   : Refuge du Couvercle
- Height difference : 700 m
- Orientation   : south
- Difficulty   : SD-GS-A
- Timing   : 2 1/2 - 3 1/2 hrs up, 45 mn down
- Time of year   : March-May
- Equipment   : as for tours on glaciers.

- **Itinerary** (photo 27)
  From the refuge, climb the steep slope alongside the south-east buttresses of the "Aiguille du Moine" onto the right branch of the "Talefre" Glacier, staying always on the right bank. Make a long, curving traverse up to the foot of the Whymper couloir "(hard to miss). It comes out to the right of the summit of the Aiguille Verte.

- **Descent**
  Same way down.

- **Note**
  You could continue up the couloir to the Aiguille Verte, but this is only for very experienced ski-mountaineers, a great classic, 600 m at an average of 47°, top 100 m at 55° (VD- EGS-A).

→
Photo 27:
33. "Refuge du Couvercle" access route - 34. to the Aiguille Verte Bergschund
35. "Col des Droite" - 36. "Pointe Isabella"

Les Droites

Col des Droites

Pointe Isabella

Col de Talèfre

Jardin
de Talèfre

Refuge du Couvercle

35

36

33

34

35 - "COL DES DROITES" (3733m)
(return trip)

Nice steep regular slope. A good introduction to steep skiing.

- Map   : IGN TOP 25 3630 OT Chamonix
- Starting point : Refuge du Couvercle
- Height difference : 1100 m
- Orientation   : South
- Difficulty   : D+ -VGS-A
- Timing   : 4-5hrs up, 1-2hrs down
- Time of year   : March-June
- Equipment   : as for tours on glaciers.

- Itinerary (photo 27)
Descend from the refuge by route n° 33, then climb east to pass under the "Jardin de Talefre" (large morained island in the shape of a heart) in the centre of the bowl. Go around it to the right and cross up north, slightly left, towards the wide slopes of the "Col des Droites". Cross the bergschund on its left and come progressively back right to climb the very steep slopes up to the col.

- Descent
Same way down, 400 m at about 40°.

- Safety tips
South facing, this gets the sun early, and after a nice cold night is often a good place to practice steep skiing. To get the best conditions wait until the surface of the snow melts to begin your descent.

36 - "POINTE ISABELLA" (3761m)
(return trip)

The most classic route in this section, the last part is not always easy laisse to the point where virtually nobody takes their skis to the summit.

Map	:	IGN TOP 25 3630 OT Chamonix
Starting point	:	Refuge du Couvercle
Height difference	:	1150 m
Orientation	:	west
Difficulty	:	D+ -VGS-A, to where you leave your skis
Timing	:	4-5hrs up, 3-4hrs down
Time of year	:	March-June
Equipment	:	as for tours on glaciers.

- **Itinerary** (photos 27 and 28)
  As for the way up, tour n° 33, to the "Talefre" glacier, then up east under the "Jardin de Talefre" (a large island in the shape of a heart) in the centre of the bowl. Go around to the right, continue east to the "Glacier des Courtes". Avoid the crevasses on the left, pass under "Les Courtes", and climb the right bank of the glacier to a small plateau (3400 m, some years a crevasse can bar the access). Traverse the plateau to the base of a rock ridge at the point marked 3401m, where you would normally leave your skis. Climb this steep snowy ridge, with rocks in places, to the "Plateau de Triolet", then to "Col de Triolet" on easy slopes. Reach the summit by the north-east ridge on steep mixed rock and snow.

- **Descent**: as for the route up.

- **Variation**
  In the Talefre bowl, you can also climb the Col de Talefre, between the Pointe des Papillons and the Pointe de Savoie. Nice route, not often done, which finishes with a steep couloir (200 m at 45°).

- **Safety tips**
  The route shown on the map hasn't been possible these last few years.

Pointe Isabella

36

to the refuge du Couvercle

ARGENTIÈRE
LE TOUR

The Argentière basin is probably one of the most frequented areas by ski tourers in the Mont Blanc chain. There are two reasons for this, firstly it's the departure point of the famous Chamonix- Zermatt (the high route), secondly it is accessible, without too much effort, by the lifts of the Grands Montets ski resort. The presence of a large, comfortable, modern refuge only adds to the attraction of this splendid valley, dominated by the north faces of the Courtes, the Droites and the Aiguille Verte. Le Tour village, very close, offers a nice ski area, mostly easy and sunny.

←

Photo 28:
36. "Pointe Isabella"

Access

Argentière is 7 kms away from Chamonix, towards Switzerland.
- By car: From Chamonix, follow Martigny.
- By Train: To Argentiére station.
- Bus: From Chamonix.
Le Tour is a few km from Argentiere, towards the Col des Montets, then right.

Lodgings

Many Hotels and Gites, ask at the Tourist office.
- Gite Le Belvedère: 04 50 54 02 59.
- Gite La Boerne: 04 50 54 05 14.
- Gite Les Moulins: 04 50 54 05 37.

Refuges

Argentiere, CAF, 150 places, always open, manned from the beginning of February: 04 50 53 16 92. Guardian: 04 50 54 62 51.
Albert 1er, CAF, manned the weekends of May on demand, 153 places, winter refuge 30 places: 04 50 54 06 20.

Useful addresses

- Grands Montets ski lifts: 04 50 54 00 71.
- Le Tour ski lifts: 04 50 54 00 58.
- Tourist office: 04 50 54 02 14.
- Ski rental, Sportech: 04 50 54 06 74. Stamos: 04 50 54 06 32.
- SNCF Train timetables: 08 36 35 35 35.
- Taxi: 04 50 93 61 47.
- Bus SAT: 04 50 78 05 33.

Ski lifts

The Grands Montets: Open from November (weekends if there is early snow), to mid May, Immense off piste ski possibilities, the top station is the starting point for many one day ski tours.

37 - LE REFUGE D'ARGENTIERE (2771m).
(hut access)

A modern building, at the foot of some of the best north faces in the Alps.

Map	:	IGN TOP 25 3630 OT Chamonix
Starting point	:	Grands Montets cable car
Height difference	:	680 m down, 220m up
Orientation	:	North-East then North-West
Difficulty	:	E-GS-A
Timing	:	1hr30-2hrs30
Time of year	:	December - mid May
Equipment	:	as for tours on glaciers.

Itinerary (photos 30 and 31)
From the top station, ski 300 hundred metres down the black piste "Point de Vue", go under the ropes to the right (on the map it's indicated to the left). Ski to the right of a large solitary rock (le Rognon, point marked 3000 m), and straight down the vast slopes of the "Rognon" Glacier. Around 2750 m, at the top of the "Moraine des Rognons", go right. The slope closes to form a wide bowl down to the Argentière Glacier. Ski progressively up and across the glacier to reach its right bank. Pass under the "Glacier du Milieu", which comes off the "Aiguille d'Argentière", then up the moraine to the refuge.

Descent
Same way down to begin with, then around 2600 m, ski down the left side of the glacier to 2300 m where the seracs start to form. Ski left onto the moraine and down to join the black piste "Point de Vue" which takes you back to Lognan (cable car mid-station) then take the red piste to the right "Le Pierre à Ric" down to Argentière (This is the route up when the lifts are closed).

- Safety tips:
- During the ski season, the ski patrol trigger all the slopes leading down t
  the glacier after every heavy snowfall, which can make the ski down ver
  dangerous, ask at the refuge before you leave.
- From the top, many tracks lead right under the Aiguille Verte and cut throu
  gh, fairly high up, the seracs of the Glacier Des Rognons, to arrive nea
  2850m, a rock island (Rognon de la Verte). These gain time and distance o
  the Argentiere glacier, but only go on excellent snow cover (many, man
  crevasses). There is always a danger of falling seracs! (photo 29).

Photo 29
37. Refuge d'Argentière
37a. Variation of the access to the refuge - 45. Col du Passor

Aiguille des
Grands Montets

Pointe coté 3000

37

37a

37a

37a

45

38 - LA FACE NORD DES COURTES (3856m)
(return trip)

Oone of the great routes, commiting, only for top flight ski mountaineers.

- Map   : IGN TOP 25 3630 OT Chamonix
- Starting point   : Refuge d'Argentière
- Height difference : 1150 m
- Orientation   : North-East
- Difficulty   : VD+ -VGS-A
- Timing   : 4hrs up
- Time of year   : March-July
- Equipment   : as for tours on glaciers.

- **Itinerary** (photos 30 and 31)
  From the refuge, down onto the glacier, then up it (south-east) to the enormous north-east couloir of the "Courtes". Climb the bottom cone to the left, then over the bergschrund on its right, up you go. Go to the right after the snow shoulder (mid-way) to the summit.

- **Descent**
  Same way down, 45-50° on the top section, and just above the Bergschrund.

→
Photo 30:
38. North-east couloir of the Courtes
39. Col des Cristaux

Les Droites

Les Courtes

Col des
Cristaux

to the Refuge d'Argentière

(38)

(39)

39 - LE COL DES CRISTAUX (3601m)
(return trip)

Not as steep as the N-E des Courtes.

- Map : IGN TOP 25 3630 OT Chamonix
- Starting point : Refuge d'Argentière
- Height difference : 900 m
- Orientation : north-east
- Difficulty : VD-EGS-A
- Timing : 4hrs up, 1-1hr30 down
- Time of year : March-June
- Equipment : as for tours on glaciers.

- **Itinerary** (photos 30 and 31)
  Down onto the glacier, then up south-east, past the Courtes, to the base of the couloir which leads up to the pass. Go a little to the right near the top (less steep).

- **Descent**: As for the way up (45° on average).

40 - LE COL D'ARGENTIERE (3552m)
(return trip)

A complete route, more difficult but less frequented than the "Col du Tour Noir" and a superb view over the Swiss side.

Map	:	IGN TOP 25 3630 OT Chamonix
Starting point	:	Refuge d'Argentière
Height difference	:	850 m
Orientation	:	SD-GS-A
Difficulty	:	west
Timing	:	3-4hrs up, 1hr down
Time of year	:	February-May
Equipment	:	as for tours on glaciers.

- Itinerary (photo 31)

From the refuge, down onto the glacier, which you skin up on the right bank along the moraine. Past the "Amethyst" Glacier, then left up the "Tour Noir" Glacier on its right bank. Around 3100 m traverse rightwards to avoid a crevassed zone then go back left and up a steep slope next to a rock spur (difficult when the snow is hard; exposed to serac fall), then move up across on easier stuff to the col.

- Descent: Same way down.

41 - LE COL DU TOUR NOIR (3535m)
(return trip)

A pleasant route opposite the north face monsters. Ideal for beginners.

- Map : IGN TOP 25 3639 OT Chamonix
- Starting point : Refuge d'Argentière
- Height difference : 760 m
- Orientation : south-west
- Difficulty : E-IMS-A
- Timing : 2-3hrs up, 30-45min down
- Time of year : February-May
- Equipment : as for tours on glaciers.

- **Itinerary** (photo 30)
Climb the steep slopes above the refuge, then go to the right up alongside the moraine of the "Amethystes" Glacier, then up a short steep slope (bordered to the right by seracs and crevasses), onto the glacier. On easier slopes go up the right bank of the glacier to the col.

- **Descent**: Same way down. If you are going back to Lognon (cable car mid-station), stay on the right side of the Amethystes Glacier.

- **Variation**: If you're coming up from Argentiere in the morning it is not necessary to go to the hut; climb directly up the right bank of the Amethystes Glacier. If you go down its left side, you can rejoin the route by traversing right around 3100 m.

- **Safety tips**: A tour like this is reasonably safe, but always have a good look around at the terrain, the danger could be above you! A lot of people stop on the large flat area at 3200 m, DON'T. Its dominated by the Y couloir of the Aiguille d'Argentière and this avalanches naturally, especially after fresh snow and/or sunny warm afternoons.

Photo 31: access to the refuge of Argentière
38, 39. towards the north-east face of the Courtes and the Col des Cristaux
40. Col d'Argentière - 41. Col du Tour Noir - 41a. Variation of the descent
42. Aiguille d'Argentière (Glacier du Milieu) - 43, 44. Col du Chardonnet, les Trois Cols

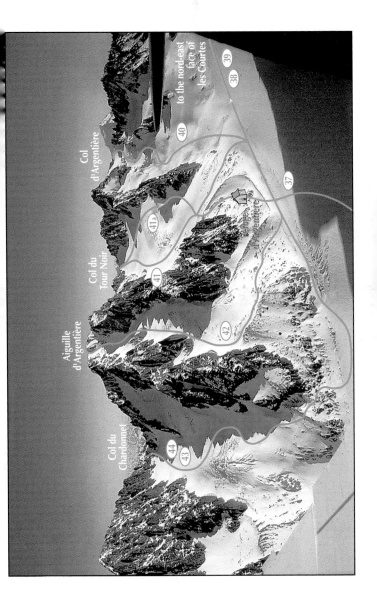

Col du
Chardonnet

Aiguille
d'Argentière

Col du
Tour Noir

Col
d'Argentière

to the nord-east
face of
les Courtes

44
43

42

41

41c

40

38
39

37

42 - L'AIGUILLE D'ARGENTIERE (3902m)
(return trip)

Classic route, steep and technical in places, not to be missed.

- Map   : IGN TOP 25 3630 OT Chamonix
- Starting point   : Refuge d'Argentiere
- Height difference : about 1220 m
- Orientation   : south-west
- Difficulty   : D-VGS-A
- Timing   : 4 - 5hrs up
- Time of year   : March-June
- Equipment   : as for tours on glaciers.

- **Itinerary** (photo 31)
  From the refuge, back down onto the "Argentiere" Glacier, then climb right, up the small valley coming off the "Glacier du Milieu". A little further up, cross to the left to avoid the steep tongue of the glacier. Follow its right bank till until approx. 3250 m. Come back to the middle at the base of the final slope. Cross the bergschrund and climb this wide, steep slope on foot. At around 3700m it becomes even steeper and brings you onto the ridge between the two summits of the "Aiguille d 'Argentière". Follow the fine ridge to the right to reach the summit.

- **Descent**: Same way down (43° on the top part).

43 - COL DU CHARDONNET (3323m)
(return trip)

Well frequented, especially on the way up, as most of the skiers are on their way to Trois Cols or Zermatt.

Map	:	IGN TOP 25 3630 OT Chamonix
Starting point	:	Refuge d'Agentière
Height difference	:	780 m
Orientation	:	south-west
Difficulty	:	SD-GS-.
Timing	:	3hrs30-4hrs30 up, 1hr down
Time of year	:	February-May
Equipment	:	as for tours on glaciers.

Itinerary (photo 31)
From the refuge, down onto and then down the "Argentière" Glacier by its right bank. Go around the "Stratton" ridge separating the "Milieu" and "Chardonnet" glaciers. Skins on at 2560 m, then right up a small, very steep slope. After 5 or 6 delicate kick turns (harscheinen may be necessary) it shallows out. Traverse the moraine to the left onto the "Chardonnet" glacier. Climb its left bank on steep slopes, then cross to its right bank where the going gets easier, stay left to the col.

Descent: same way down, but it's better to finish by the three Cols (tour n° 44).

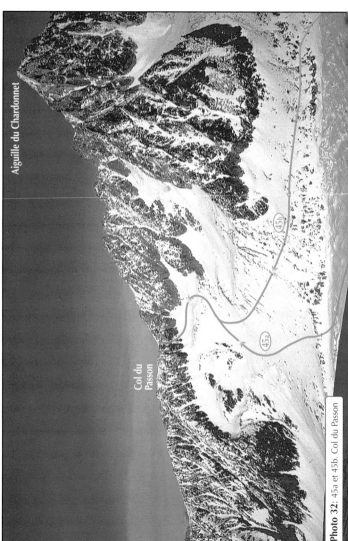

Aiguille du Chardonnet

Col du Passon

45b

45a

Photo 32: 45a et 45b. Col du Passon

Aiguille du Chardonnet

44

45

Photo 33: 44. "Les 3 cols", descent to "le Tour" - 45. Col du Passon, descent to "le Tour"

44 - LES TROIS COLS
(circuit)

The classic ski tour, very varied.

- Map   : IGN TOP 25 3630 OT Chamonix
- Starting point   : Refuge d'Argentière
- Height difference : Variable depending on your choice of itinerary, averag
                       1000 m up, 2000 m down
- Orientation   : SD-GS-A
- Difficulty   : south-west up, north-west down
- Timing   : Total 6-8hrs
- Time of year   : February-May
- Equipment   : as for tours on glaciers.

- **Itinerary** (photos 31, 39 and 41)
  As for tour n° 43 to the "Col du Chardonnet".
  Go down the east side (Swiss, 100 m at 45° and narrow, rope useful, there i
  a sling at the col and a 90 m rope is required). Continue, traversing left or
  the "Saleina" Glacier, then obliquely left just after the rock buttresses of the
  "Grande Fourche". Climb the slopes leading to the "Fenêtre de Saleina"
  Reach the col by a short steep passage. Carry on north-west under the "Tête
  Blanche", then up several dozen metres to the left to arrive at the "Col du
  Tour".

- **Descent** (photo 33 and 34)
  From the "Col du Tour", down the Glacier "du Tour" staying left, under an
  isolated rocky outcrop (point marked 3238 m), then down the left bank of
  the glacier. Near 2750 m, ski down the gully to the right of the rock spur
  (point marked 2722 m) staying left of the seracs. Down the steep slopes that
  follow, working slightly left to 2300 m. Descend the moraine on the left and

→
Photo 34

44. "Les 3 cols" - 44a. "Fenêtre du Tour - 45. Col du passon descen
46. to Albert 1er refuge - 46a. From the "Col du Passon" to Albert 1er - 48. Aiguille du Tour circui

126

keep working left to pass under the base of a huge rock shoulder ("Le Bec de la Cluy", 2334 m). Still traversing left, go down some steep slopes under the "Tête du Grand Chantet", to reach the top of the larch forest. Then down on the right next to the edge of the forest towards "Le Tour". At about 1600 m this becomes very steep so come back to the left (still steep, but avoids the rock barriers, difficult to find) and on to the village by traversing towards the right.

- Variations
- From the "Fenêtre de Saleina" there is a classic variant, which consists of skiing down to the swiss village of "Trient" (see tour n° 54). But you have to organise your way back (bus, then train or taxi).
- From the "col du Chardonnet" you can climb directly to the "fenêtre du Tour", situated to the left of the Grande Fourche. This shorter passage brings you directly onto the top part of the Tour Glacier.

- Safety tips
- Make sure you do this route in good weather, the way back to the village is very difficult in poor visibility.
- The north face of the Aiguille d'Argentière is overhung by menacing seracs.
- See also "Safety tips" tour n° 45.

45 - COL DU PASSON (3028m)
(circuit)

⊏airly technical route, a good ski down for the climb.

Map	: IGN TOP 25 3630 OT Chamonix
Starting point	: Grands Montets top station
Height difference	: 750 m up, 2500 m down
Orientation	: north-east then south- west to the Col, north -west down
Difficulty	: D-S-A
Timing	: 5-6hrs in all
Time of year	: January-May
Equipment	: as for tours on glaciers.

- **Itinerary** (photos 29 and 32)
  - From the Grand Montets top station**:** follow route 37 down to the Argentiere glacier. Traverse straight across the flat glacial plateau to reach the moraine on the right bank. Make a long rising traverse left under the west face of the "Aiguille de Chardonnet".
  From the last flat area a long traverse to the left brings you to the bottom of the couloirs (100 m at 35°/40°). The finish is steep and narrow, sometimes icy(crampons are useful)
  - Variation 45a: when snow conditions are safe.

- **Descent** (photo 33 and 34)
  From the col go down the Tour glacier towards the north, then traverse left to the top of the gully to the right of the rock spur marked 2722 m. From here as for tour n° 44 to the Tour village.

- **Variations** (photo 36)
  - *Col Superior Adams Reilly (3478 m).*
  From the "col du Passon", after descending the first slope climb back up to the right passing under the Aiguille de Passon. You will arrive on the upper part of the "glacier du Tour". Go up its left bank until you see the rocky island, point marked 3214 m. Climb the short steep slope to its left and follow the glacier as best as you can between the crevasses. The "col Adams Reilly" is

at the foot of the west ridge of the Aiguille du Chardonnet.
- Descend by the same route, (D-GS-A).

- *Descent on the Glacier des Grands in Switzerland:*
  From the col, traverse the glacier du Tour and climb up to the Albert 1er refuge. Go north-east above the hut to the point marked 3094 m, then follow tou n° 54.

- Safety tips
  The bottom part of the route down as we describe it is the safest. Often you will see numerous tracks going off right into steep couloirs to come out at the "Gratapia". This route follows a series of gullies dominated by polished rock slabs, not much for the snow to stick to, only to be done in the right conditions.

46 - "REFUGE ALBERT 1ᴱᴿ" (2702m)
(hut access)

The summer route from "le Tour", described here, isn't the safest in winter, better to come down from Switzerland or Argentière.

- Map : IGN TOP25 3630 OT Chamonix
- Starting point : Le Tour
- Height difference : 1250 m
- Orientation : west
- Difficulty : SD-BS
- Timing : 4-6hrs up
- Time of year : depends on the snow cover
- Equipment : as fot tours on glaciers.

- **Itinerary** (photo 34)
  Go right, up the grassy slopes from the bottom of the Charamillon lift station, following the summer path on foot. This goes up a steep couloir and then well round to the left of the "Cascade de Pichieu". You arrive at around 2000 m, near an EDF building, in a large bowl bordered to the right by a moraine. Follow this all the way to the refuge.

- **Safety tips**
  - Not to be undertaken when there is still snow below 2000 m, access from the "col du Passon" is advised earlier in the season (tour n° 45). When conditions allow it is also possible to reach the hut by climbing route 45 from Le Tour village and traversing the glacier leftwards above the icefall.
  - We do not advise the access on ski from the Charamillon telecabine and the traverse under the Bec du Picheu. Even if it is marked on the map it is too risky.

47 - "AIGUILLE DU TOUR" (3542m)
By the "Couloir de la Table"
(return trip)

Good introduction to steeps.

- Map   : IGN TOP 25 3630 OT Chamonix
- Starting point   : Refuge Albert 1er
- Height difference : 1250m
- Orientation   : west
- Difficulty   : VD- VGS-A
- Timing   : 3-4hrs up, 1hr down
- Time of year   : March-June
- Equipment   : as for tours on glaciers.

- **Itinerary** (photo 35)
From the refuge, go down onto the Tour glacier, climb up its right bank and traverse up above the "Signal Reilly" (rock spur). Go slightly towards the right, then at about 3100 m, come back left in the direction of the south face of the "Aiguille du Tour". Climb up the "Couloir de la Table" (dominated by a large balanced block) to a small col. From here a short technical climb gets you onto the summit if you want.

- **Descent**: Same way down (200 m at 45°, steeper at the beginning).

→
Photo 35:
47. Aiguille du Tour, "couloir de la Table"
48. Aiguille du Tour: circuit
49. Towards the "col du Tour", Tête Blanche and Petite Fourche

Aiguille
du Tour

Col supérieur
du Tour

47

48

49

to the
hutte

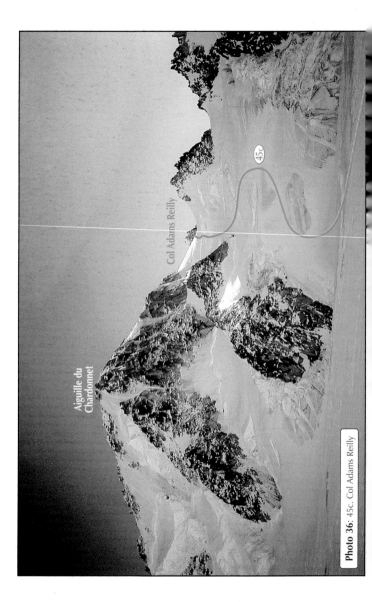

Aiguille du Chardonnet

Col Adams Reilly

45c

Photo 36: 45c. Col Adams Reilly

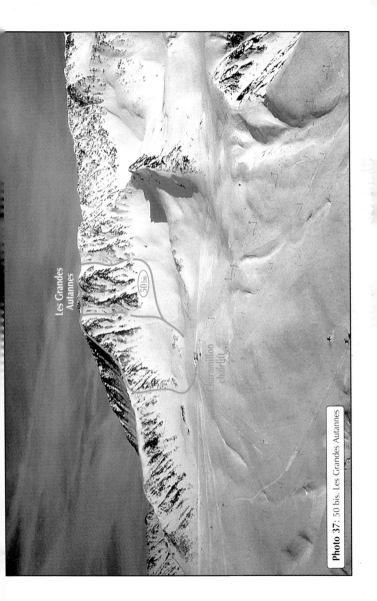

Les Grandes Autannes

50 bis

Charamillon chairlift

Photo 37 : 50 bis. Les Grandes Autannes

48 - AIGUILLE DU TOUR CIRCUIT (3542m)

Takes you round a variety of differing mountainsides.

- Map   : IGN TOP 25 3630 OT Chamonix
- Starting point   : Refuge Albert 1er
- Height difference   : 650 m up
- Orientation   : west then east then west again
- Difficulty   : SD-IMS-A
- Timing   : 3 - 4hrs
- Time of year   : March-June.

- **Itinerary** (photo 34 ,35 and 38)
  From the refuge, go down onto the Tour glacier, climb up its right bank and traverse up above the "Signal Reilly" (rock spur). Continue traversing up south and climb the second glacial bay to the left between two ridges to the "Col Superior du Tour" (3289 m). Once in Switzerland go north, past the foot of the "Aiguille Purtscheller" (short steep passage), then to the foot of the "Aiguille du Tour". Go a little further to where the slope starts to descend and off with your skins.

- **Descent**:
  Ski down a little then traverse left and through the notch between the "Aiguille du Pissoir" and the "Aiguille du Midi des Grands". Then obliquely to the left and over the "Col du Midi des Grands". Follow the middle of the glacier to begin with, then to the left to the "Signal Reilly" and easily back to the refuge.

→

Photo 38:
48. Aiguille du tour circuit
54. "Glacier de Bron"
54a. "Glaciers des Grands"

- Variations
  - Go the other way round.
  - Climb the Aiguille du Tour, (3542 m).
  From directly below the summit go left up a steep snow slope, then climb (or
  foot) the south-east ridge on easy rock.
  - You could also go down to Trient on the glacier "Des Grands" (see tour n°
    54).

- Safety tips:
  Attention, you are in two countries, the contour lines on the IGN (French)
  maps changes after the white band near the border. On the Swiss part they
  go from 10 m to 20 m. The OFT (Swiss) maps keep the same distance in all
  countries.

→
Photo 39:
44. "Les 3 cols" - 52. "Cabane du Trient"
52a. "Glacier du Trient" descent
52a. toward "glacier de Bron" and "Glacier des Grands"
54. "Aiguilles Dorées" circuit

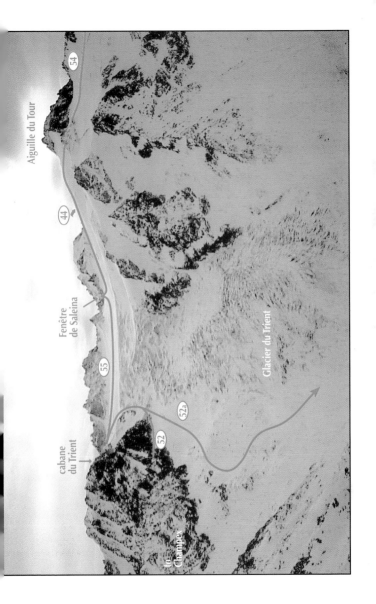

49 - TETE BLANCHE (3429m) - PETIT FOURCHE (3520m)
(return trip)

Two nice little summits, also easily accessible from the Trient refuge.

- Map   : IGN TOP 25 3630 OT Chamonix
- Starting point   : Refuge Albert 1er
- Height difference : 850 m
- Orientation   : north-west
- Difficulty   : D-GS-A, (E-IMS-A, for the Tête Blanche)
- Timing   : 3-4hrs up, 1hr down
- Time of year   : March-June
- Equipment   : as for tours on glaciers.

- **Itinerary** (photos 34 and 35)
  From the refuge follow route 48 until it heads left to the "col Superieur du Tour". Continue traversing up towards the south in the direction of the "Col du Tour". Around 3200 m go right, leaving the "col du Tour" on your left. Keep going to the south, climb a steep slope to reach a shoulder (above the marked point 3238 m). Cross to the left to gain easily the "Tête Blanche".
  From there, easily down to the "Col Blanc", then climb a steep slope (100 m at 40°) which brings you onto the ridge of the "Petite Fourche". Up some rocks to the left to the summit.

- **Descent**: By the same route.

- **Variation**
  The north face of the Tête Blanche (150 m at 50°) is a very good place to practice extreme skiing.

50 - "COL DES AUTANNES" (2777m)
and the "Glacier de Bron"
(traverse)

A not very obvious col on the border which gives access to the north slopes of the Trient valleys.

Map	: IGN TOP 25 3630 OT Chamonix
Starting point	: Teleseige du Col du Balme
Height difference	: 560 m up, 1400 m down
Orientation	: up west, north down
Difficulty	: D-VGS
Timing	: 2-2hrs30 up
Time of year	: January-April
Equipment	: as for tours on glaciers.

Itinerary
From the top of the chairlift go south, by a long slightly descending traverse, and pass the bottom of spur of the "petite Tête de Charamillon". After arriving at a flat area, go east to pass the "Lac de Charamillon"(not visible) and climb up the sustained slopes towards the col.

Descent
From the col, down onto the "glacier de Bron" which you reach either by an arc shaped bowl or by cutting across the small ridge on the right. Stay right, to the Trient valley. From the "Cabane" (1583 m) follow the road to the village.

Safety tips:
Very avalanche prone, only to be undertaken in excellent conditions, crampons useful on the way up to the col.

50 bis - "LES GRANDES AUTANNES" (2680m)
(return trip)

Some great slopes, easily accessible from the Tour ski resort.

- Map   : IGN TOP 25 3630 OT Chamonix
- Starting point   : Le Tour
- Height difference : 500m up, 1200m down
- Orientation   : west
- Difficulty   : D-VGS
- Timing   : 2-2hrs30 up, 1hr down
- Time of year   : January-April.

- **Itinerary** (photo 37)
  From the top of the teleseige go to the Col de Balme and join directly the North ridge of the Grandes Autannes, which you follow to the summit.

- **Descent**
  Straight down the slope, composed of many small gullys. Steep but regular.

- **Safety tips**
  Try not to set off avalanches onto the pistes!

A new automatic avalanche triggering system which has been installed on the north ridge may mean that this route is no longer possible.

VALAIS Area
(Swiss)

The west part of the Mont Blanc chain is shared between three countrie France, Switzerland and Italy. With large glacial plateaus (Trient, Le Tou Saleina), accessible between them by high cols; it is without a doubt the be adapted area for ski touring. The valaisian side of the Mont Blanc chain is art culated around several valleys and villages, Le Chatelard, Trient and above a the Val Ferret. Very few ski lifts in this section just a few family resort Champex, La Fouly. But many high mountain refuges are dotted about, wit the advantages of the Swiss refuges, which are not always manned during th ski season, but always supplied with blankets, kitchen and cooking equipmen

Access

By car: from Chamonix, direction Martigny, then from there towards the "Co du Grand St Bernard" to Orsieres, then to La Fouly or Champex.
By Train or Bus: Chamonix to Martigny, then Orsieres, then La Fouly o Champex.
Don't forget your passports.

Lodgings

Many Hotels in the villages, some with cheap dormitories.
- Hotel des Glaciers in La Fouly, 027 783 11 71.
- Hotel Eidelweiss (la Fouly), 027 783 26 21.
- Auberge de jeunesse (Champex), 027 783 14 23.
- Auberge du Val d'Arpette (Champex), 027 783 12 21.

Refuges

- **Cabane d'Orny (2381 m)**: CAS, manned in summer, 80 places; 027 783 18 87
- **Cabane de Trient (3170)**: CAS, always open, manned from mid March-May, 140 places, 027 783 14 38.
- **Cabane de Saleina (2691)**: CAS, always open, not manned in spring, wood and kitchen equipment, 027 783 17 00.
- **"Refuge de l'Envers des Dorées" (Plines) (2980 m)**: Not manned, 11 places open all year, no gas.
  Part accessible by reservation: 021 921 85 50, 12 places, equipped kitchen.

"Cabane de l'A Neuve" (2785 m): CAS, 30 places, always open, manned in spring,
027 783 24 24
Refuge bivouac Cesare Fiorio (2724 m): CAI, 16 places, blankets and mattresses.
Next to it is another small rustic cabin with 4 places, (Bivouac du Dolent).

ki lifts / useful addresses

Tel. prefixe for swizerland 41

Champex: Small resort with 3 lifts

La Fouly: Nice setting with 4 lifts

Mountain rescue: 1414 or 144.

Distress frequency: Channel K 158 625 - Channel E 161 300

Champex tourist Office: 027 783 12 27

Guides office La Fouly: 027 783 29 49

La Fouly Tourism Office: 027783 27 17

- Orsieres Bus Station: 0041 (0) 27 783 11 05 or 27 783 11 43

- Weather, Haute Savoie: 157 126 265.

- Swiss French Alp: 157 126 248.

- Internet: http://www.meteosuisse.ch

- Snow and avalanche bulletin: 187.

- Internet http://www.slf.ch/slf.htlm.

Starting Points

- Col de la Forclaz: On the Chamonix-Martigny road, after Trient, car park at the col.
- Champex: From Champex downtown go up to "Champex d'en Haut" and park at the "la Brey" chairlift.
- La Fouly: At the end of the swiss Val Ferret, carpark near the lifts.

51 - "POINTE RONDE" (2700m)
(circuit or return trip)

Lovely north slopes, often in powder, which take you to an exceptional view point on the Swiss side of the chain.

- Map   : IGN TOP 25 3630 OT Chamonix
- Starting point   : Col de la Forclaz
- Height difference : 1170 m
- Orientation   : north then north-east
- Difficulty   : SD-GS
- Timing   : 4-5hrs up, 1hr30-2hrs down
- Time of year   : December-April

- **Itinerary** (photo 40)
From the Forclaz Pass go towards the east on the Martigny side (sign post marked Bovine), follow the forest path through several clearings, traverse the steep "Combe des Faces" to come out of the forest at about 1850 m in a clearing near the "Chalets de la Giete" (1884 m). Go up south-east and climb the steep bowl to the col at 2260 m. Follow the small valley to the right which shrinks at the top to form the north-east ridge of the "Pointe Rond" to the summit (stay mainly on the east side).

- **Descent**: Same way down.
  - Or by the north face: (La Veudale), come a few metres back down the ridge then traverse left onto the north face to follow one of the narrow gullies (40°). Navigate as best as you can between the rocks to reach the wide open slopes which you go down on the left.
  At the forest level traverse to the right to meet the path. Then back to the "Col de la Forclaz.
  - With good snow cover ski down the bowl ("combe des Faces") to "la Caffe" (3,5 km back to the col).

→
Photo 40:
51. "pointe Ronde"

Pointe Ronde

51

vers
la Caffe

vers
le Col de la Forclaz

- Variation
- From the unnamed col (2660 m) you can also climb the "Genepi" (2829 m).
- This route is also feasible from the Chalets de la Caffe.

- Safety tips

A rope could be useful for the first few metres of the north face.

There is sometimes an avalanche risk on the traverse from the "Col de l Fourche", in which case you should take the route up from the "Chalets d la Caffe".

→

Photo 41:
44. "Les 3 Cols"
52a. Ravines Rousses glacier
53, 53a and 53b. Toward "Cabane de Saleina"
55. "Aiguilles Dorées" circuit - 57a. Towards "Col de la Grande Lui"
57b. Towards "La Grande Lui", west couloir

Grande Fourche

Fenêtre de Saleina

Aiguilles Dorées

bivouac
de Plines

toward Col
du Chardonnet

toward
la Grande Lui

44

53a

55

53b

52a

53

57a

57b

52 - "CABANE DU TRIENT"
(hut access)

Situated on the Chamonix-Zermatt route, next to the Trient glacial plateau, this cosy refuge has few visitors in winter. Starting point of some very pretty glacial traverses (Trois cols Suisse, Tour des Dorées, Tour des Aiguilles du Tour) it also offers some grand descents. Stable snow conditions are required for this route.

- Map : IGN TOP 25 3630 OT Chamonix, CN Suisse 1345 Orsiere
- Starting point : Champex
- Height difference : 1600 m
- Orientation : east
- Difficulty : SD-GS-A
- Timing : 6-7hrs up, 2hrs down
- Time of year : March-May
- Equipment : as for tours on glaciers.

- **Itinerary** (photo 39)
  - From the Breya chairlift carpark go up the road to the right to the "Arpette". Follow the valley's right bank up to 2250 m, then cross left and up the "Combe des Ecandies". On good snow, climb the steep slopes up to the "Col des Ecandies" and onto the "Trient" Glacier. Go up the right bank of the glacier alongside the "Point d'Orny" to the refuge, built on a rocky spur. If the snow cover is bad, climb the steep couloir to the left of the "col des Ecandies". This "Brêche de la Fenêtre des Chamois" is not named on the map. A sideways traverse gets us back on route.
  - From the Argentiere glacier side: combine routes 44, 46a and 48.

Descents

- By the "Val d'Arpette": same way down.
- By the "Combe d'Orny": from the refuge, descend briefly south to the Col d'Orny, and down the "glacier d'Orny" on its left bank, underneath the "Orny" hut to where at 2600 m the glacier forms an elbow to the right. Leave it by the left (short climb) and go around the point marked 2630 m on the right. Traverse right to join the "Combe de la Lui des Revers", then the north slopes under the "Chatelet". Come back to the bowl around 1650 m and ski the valley (tricky if little snow).

Then either, near 1400 m, traverse left and follow the traces of a forest path which take you to Champex or, around 1200 m there is another forest path to the right which brings you to the road to Fouly (bus or taxi back to Champex).

- By the Trient Glacier, (VGS): a very interesting north face descent; needs good snow cover. From the refuge go down the right side of the Trient glacier. Ski carefully the steep slopes under the "Petite Pointe d'Orny", always staying to the right side, leaving to the right the "Col des Ecandies".

At around 2600 m leave the glacier and ski the obvious bowl. At the place called "Versevay" (2096 m), come back towards the glacier skiing close to some waterfalls. Go down the the valley to the building at 1580 m and follow the route 54.

- By the "Glacier des Plines", (see tour n° 55).
- By the "Glacier de Ravine Rousse", VGS. A spring heliski route.

From the refuge look for the "Roc des Plines" (3294 m). From the "Col d'Orny" go up to the south-west, following the rupture line between the "glacier d'Orny" and the Trient plateau. Go over the "Col Droit" (often corniced) and down the first steep slope. Follow the vague snowy ridge to the south-east, then near 3100 m turn left onto wide slopes. Several obvious and steep couloirs bring you down onto the Saleina glacier (photo 41).

Avoid the last part of the glacier if there is not enought snow.

Go around by the left, near 2050 m, on sustained slopes to the "Vallon d'Arpette". On good snow cover ski down to the end of the glacier.

- **Safety tips**:

  The access to the "Combe d'Orny" from the top of the Breya chairlift is definitely not advised. It crosses south-east slopes which are steep and exposed to avalanches. If necessary it can be done when the snow has completely melted. But in this case the lift will generally be closed.

→

Photo 42:
56. "Cabane de L'A Neuve"
57. Grande Lui
58. The Swiss "Trois Cols"

53 - "CABANE DE SALEINA" (2691m)
(hut access)

A new, pleasant, replacement for the old refuge, situated on a rock spu[r] which dominates the "Glacier de Saleina". Only reachable on skis from above.

- Map : IGN TOP25 3630 OT Chamonix
  or Swiss map: 1345 Orsieres
- Starting point : 1) Refuge d'Argentiere (tour n° 37)
  2) Cabane de Trient (tour n° 52)
- Height difference : 1) 880m up, 740m down
  2) 200m up, 670m down
- Orientation : 1) east then north-east.
  2) north then south-east then north-east
- Difficulty : 1) SD-GS-A. 2) E-IMS-A
- Timing : 1) 4hrs30-5hrs30 total
  2) 2-3hrs total
- Time of year : March-May
- Equipment : as for tours on glaciers.

- Itineraries (photos 41 and 43)

1) From the "refuge d'Argentiere" follow route n° 43 to the "Col du Chardonnet". From there go down the centre of the "Glacier de Saleina", avoiding the seracs on the left, then go over onto its right bank at about 2900 m.

Around 2600m, before a highly crevassed zone, leave the glacier by the right and traverse up to the refuge (fairly steep).

2) From the "Cabane du Trient",

a- by the "Fenêtre de Saleina": Traverse the Trient plateau to the south-west (under the Aiguilles Dorées north side) and through the "Fenetre de Saleina".

→

Photo 43:
53. "Cabane de Saleina"
57a. Towards "la Grande Lui" pass
58. The Swiss"3 Cols"

Grand Combin

cabane de Saleina

57a

58

53

Descend the Saleina glacier and go over to its right side, then follow the same route description as above.

b- by the "Col Droit". Same start as tour n° 52. After the steep slopes on the south side of the "col Droit" go to the right and ski the wide slopes down to the glacier.

- Safety tips

Unmanned in spring, the Cabane is mainly used as a stage on the traverse of the "Combe de l'A Neuve" by the three cols Swiss (tour n° 58). Try not to get blocked by bad weather because the Val Ferret descent is not easy. But, if you do, it is better to come down the left bank of the Saleina Glacier to the "Vallon d'Arpette" and the village "Praz de Fort". The summer path to Praz de Fort is impossible when snowed over, chains, ladders, slab, etc...

54 - "GLACIER DE BRON ET DES GRANDS"
(traverse)

Great glacial routes which attract heliskiers.

Map	: IGN TOP 25 3630 OT Chamonix.Swiss map 1324 Barberine, 1325 Sembrancher, 1344 Col de Balme or 1345 Orsieres
Starting point	: Cabane de Trient. Also accessible from "refuge Albert 1er", tour 46 and 48 or Refuge "d'Argentiere" (tour 44) or Col de Passon (tour 45)
Height difference	: 220 m up, 2000m down
Orientation	: north-east
Difficulty	: E-GS-A
Timing	: 3-4hrs total
Time of year	: March-May
Equipment	: as for tours on glaciers.

Itinerary (photos 38 and 39)

From the "Cabane du Trient", down onto and west across the plateau towards the "Aiguille du Tour" (Count 1hr extra if you want to climb it). Up some steeper slopes and over a small col to the right of the "l'Aiguille du Pissoir". Down the "glacier des Grands", keeping left alongside the rocks of the "Aiguille du Midi des Grands" to about 3000 m. Traverse horizontally left completely across the top of the Grands glacier. Go down its left side to near the "Croix de Bron" (2898 m). After this passage descend the "Glacier de Bron" and the valley it follows. Near 2000 m this shrinks into a closed in couloir which takes you to the bottom of the Trient valley. At around 1580 m, next to a chalet, take the forest path on the left to Trient (buses and taxis).

- Variations

There are many descent variations onto the "Glacier des Grands". Avoid the steep right bank of the glacier which is avalanche prone.
The left side variations are safest.

- Safety tips

Most of the routes on this side are prone to slab avalanches after fresh snow the last part is a real trap! Check conditions!

Photo 44:
56a. "Cabane de L'A Neuve"
57. Towards "Grande Lui"
58. The Swiss "3 cols" (col des Essettes)

La Fouly

cabane
de l'A Neuve

56

58

57

55 - "AIGUILLES DOREES TOUR"
(circuit)

A circuit in a quiet corner of the chain, the new "Envers des Dorées" bivoua hut opens up new possibilities.

- Map : IGN TOP 25 3630 OT Chamonix.
  Swiss map: 1345 Orsieres
- Starting point : Cabane de Trient
- Height difference : 600 m up and down
- Orientation : north then south-east
- Difficulty : E-IMS-A
- Timing : total 2hrs30-3hrs, total
- Time of year : March-May
- Equipment : as for tours on glaciers.

- **Itinerary** (photos 39 and 41)
  From the refuge, down onto the glacier and traverse the plateau south-wes to the "Fenetre de Saleina". Go through it and down onto the "glacier d Saleina". Go left and pass under the south ridge of the "Aiguille de l Varappe" and continue sideways to the east. Pass near to the new hut an climb up the "Glacier des Plines" towards the "Col de Droit" (right of the "Aiguilles Dorees"). Climb up the steep slope (a rope may be useful) to the pass then to the "cabane de Trient".

56 - THE "CABANE DE L'A NEUVE" (2735m)
(hut access)

One of the most adorable refuges in these mountains, perched on a spur under the Pointes des Essettes, opposite the Mont Dolent.

Map	: IGN TOP 25 3630 OT Chamonix. Swiss map 1345 Orsieres
Starting point	: La Fouly
Height difference	: 1140 m
Orientation	: east then south
Difficulty	: SD-GS-A
Timing	: 3hrs30 - 4hrs30
Time of year	: February-May
Equipment	: as for tours on glaciers.

Itinerary (photos 42 and 44)

From the carpark go down a little and cross the bridge to the right in the direction of the campsite. Climb the wide valley which goes up to the west of the village, stay on its right bank. Around 2000 m you arrive at the bottom of the glacier. Go up its left bank, then on up right on the wide sustained slopes of the "Essettes". Climb well to the left of the refuge till you come level and then traverse across. It is situated on a little rocky spur under the "Pointes des Essettes".

Descent
Same way down.

Safety tips
The summer path is impracticable when snowed over.
High avalanche risk after heavy snow.

57 - "LA GRANDE LUI" (3509m)
(return trip)

A major route of the chain... A real, pure, pleasure, on good snow.

- Map   : IGN TOP 25 3630 OT Chamonix.
                         Swiss map 1345 Orsieres
- Starting point   : "Cabane de l'A Neuve"
- Height difference   : 775 m
- Orientation   : south-east
- Difficulty   : SD-GS-A
- Timing   : 2hrs30-3hrs up, 45min down
- Time of year   : February-May
- Equipment   : as for tours on glaciers.

- **Itinerary** (photos 42, 44)
  From the refuge go horizontally to the west, then up some wide slopes.
  Around 3040 m go to the right of the rock (rognon), then cross up left toward
  the "Grande Lui". Leave your skis at the bottom of the last steep slope which
  leads up to the "Col de la Grande Lui" (3419 m), immediately to the right of
  the summit. Get to the top by the east ridge (mixed).

- **Descent**:
  - same way down.
  - central couloir on the south face, (EGS-A) not very obvious, often cluttered
    by exposed rock.

- **Variations**
  - Grande Lui by the north-west side via the "col de la Grande Lui", from the
    Argentiere Hut. See route 37 and 44 (photos 41 and 43).
  - By the west couloir (250 m at 45°, D-EGS-A).
  - Traverse to the Col de l'A Neuve (3403m).

- **Safety tips**: On the Chamonix map IGN 3630 OT Chamonix, the SCaleina
  and Grande Lui Cols have been switched so the ski route to the col marked
  3390 m is false. The Swiss map is correct.

58 - THE SWISS "TROIS COLS"
(circuit)

An original route across small glaciers with few visitors, one of our favourite routes.

Map	: IGN TOP 25 3630 OT Chamonix.
	Swiss map 1345 Orsieres
Starting point	: Cabane de Saleina
Height difference	: 530 m up, 1560 m down
Orientation	: north-west then south, south-east then south-west
Difficulty	: D-GS-A
Timing	: 4-6hrs total
Time of year	: March-May
Equipment	: as for tours on glaciers.

Itinerary (photos 42,43 and 44)

From the refuge traverse up towards the south-west, pass under the foot of the north-west buttresses of the "Grande Pointe des Planereuses". Then by a tricky passage (steep and exposed) to the "Col des Planereuses". From there, cross a few metres to the right and descend onto the "Glacier des Planereuses" by a short rock passage (rope 20 m). Go down to 2900 m and traverse horizontally across the glacier to avoid the crevasses. On foot, climb the steep slope to the right to the "Col superior de Crête Sèche" (3024 m, not marked on the Swiss map). Traverse the "Glacier Treutse Bo" and on up to the "Col des Essettes" (3113 m, not named on the IGN map). Descend to the l'A Neuve valley by a steep couloir. A rope is very useful to negociate one 150 m section (bolt belay on the right). Traverse right to avoid a rock barrier then back into the fall line. From where you can see the hut join itinerary 56.

- Variation
   "Le Petit Darrey" (3508 m): which you can do from the "Col des Planereuses"
   Climb the glacier du Darrey to the right.

- Safety tips
   Don't try to go directly down the Planereuses or Treutse Bo Glaciers to th
   valleys underneath, no way through.

59 - "TETE DE FERRET" (2713 m)
(return trip)

Dominates the Petit Col Ferret, ancient passage into Italy.

Map	:	IGN TOP 25 3630 OT Chamonix.
		Swiss map: 1345 Orsieres
Starting point	:	La Fouly
Height difference	:	1115 m
Orientation	:	north-east
Difficulty	:	SD-GS
Timing	:	4-4hrs30 up, 1-2hrs down
Time of year	:	December-May.

Itinerary (photos 45, 46)
Park at La Fouly, follow the "Route de Ferret" to the "Hameau du Clou". Cross the stream by the footbridge and follow the "Sentier de la Léchère". Climb up to about 1950 m, under the "Crétet de la Gouille", then traverse sideways to the "Combe des Fonds". Climb this to 2380 m, then go up the steep slopes to the left onto the north ridge, and easily up to the summit.

- **Descent**. By the same route.

- **Variation**
Carry on into Italy from the Petit Col Ferret. Drop down the steep, exposed, south side, working to the right to arrive at the base of the couloir leading to the "Maisons de Pré-le-Bar", then down the Val Ferret on the cross country tracks to Planpancieux (long and flat). There is a bus from there to La Palud.

- **Safety tips**
The bottom part of the "Combe des Fonds" is regularly swept by enormous avalanches coming off the "Mont Dolent". Although it is much shorter than the route described above it should be taken only when the snowpark is very stable.

60 - MONT DOLENT (3821m)
(return trip)

G rand glacial route to the meeting point of three countries.

- Map   : IGN TOP 25 3630 OT Chamonix.
                        Swiss map: 1345 Orsieres or 1365 Grand St Bernard
- Starting point   : La Fouly
- Height difference   : Day1) 1130 m up
                        Day2) 1100 m up, 2230m down
- Orientation   : North-East then South
- Difficulty   : D+-VGS-A
- Timing   : Day1) 4-5hrs; Day2) 4-6hrs up; 3-4hrs down
- Time of year   : March-June
- Equipment   : as for tours on glaciers.

- **Itinerary** (photos 45, 46)
  - **Day1)** As for tour n° 59, to the "Petit Col Ferret". From there, cross sideways to the right (exposed) between the rocks to go over the south ridge of the "Pointe Allobrogia" (2513 m on the Swiss map). Climb up right to get to the Cesare Fiorio (4 places and 16 places) 2724 m.
  - **Day2)** From the bivouac climb up north to the foot of the "Pointe Allobrogia" buttresses. Traverse sideways to the left under the rock ridge, then up the left bank of the "Pré-de-Bar" Glacier to about 3500 m. A succession of steep bumps (climb by the left on skis or on foot) brings you to a bowl under the summit. Generally you would leave your skis at the "Collet du Grapillon" (to the right, around 3700 m, not marked on the maps). Up the final slope and slender ridge to the summit.

→
Photo 45:
59. Tête de Ferret
59a. Variation: descent sur le Val Ferret italien
60. Le Mont Dolent

- **Descent**

  Same way down, from the "col des Grapillon"(several parts at 40°).
  The descent from the top is steep 150 m at 45° and exposed (above seracs
  only for connoisseurs.

- **Variations**

  The Mont Allobroge (3171 m) and the Petit Grepillon (3358 m) are direct
  above the refuge, making two interesting objectives.

- **Safety tips**

  The traverse towards the "Petit Col Ferret" can be very dangerous if it warm
  up! Don't hesitate to spend another night at the refuge if you get down to
  late.
  The best way back down to the left side of the Pre-de-Bar Glacier is not eas
  to find. Check it out the night before.
  The bottom part of the "Combe des Fonds" is regularly swept by enormou
  avalanches coming off the "Mont Dolent". Although it is much shorter tha
  the route described above it should be taken only when the snowpark is ver
  stable.

→

Photo 46

59 - 60. "Petit col Ferret" and "Tête de Ferret": route to the "bivouac du Dolent" (Cesare Fioric
59a - 60a. The "Combe des Fonds

VAL D'AOSTE
Area
(Italy)

Italy shares two of the highest mountains in the range with France, the Mc Blanc and the Grandes Jorasses. You have also the two valleys, Val Ferret to t north, Val Veny to the south and the little town of Courmayeur in the midd There are a lot of refuges but not many are accessible on skis.

Access

From Chamonix: by car, the Mont Blanc tunnel. If the tunnel is closed go Matigny (Switzerland) and the col du Grand Saint Bernard (toll).
Bus: from the train station (Chamonix), daily at 8.45 am (stops at La Palud f the Hellbronner lift).

Lodgings

Hotels and furnished rooms: tourist office in Coumayeur. 01 65 84 20 60
Dormitories:
- Hotel Funivia a la Palud: 01 65 89 924.
- Refuge Auberge CAI Uget: 01 65 86 90 97.

Refuges

- Elisabetta Soldini (2205 m): CAI, unmanned during the ski season, winter hu 24 places, 01 65 84 40 80.
- Torino (3371 m): at the top of the Helbronner cable car, two refuges, old one, 01 65 84 64 84. new one, 01 65 84 40 34.
- La Vachey: private, 01 65 86 97 23.
- Gonella: CAI, unmanned during the ski season, winter hut, 30 places, 01 65 88 51 01.
- "Bivouac du Petit Mont Blanc": 9 places, mattresses, blankets.
- "Bivouac d'Estelette": 3-4 places, blankets (unique. Worth a visit).

Useful addresses

- Tourist office: Courmayeur, 01 65 84 20 60.
- Helbronner cable car, 01 65 89 92 5.
- Courmayeur ski lifts, 01 65 84 66 58.
- Courmayeur Guides bureau, 01 65 84 20 64 or 01 65 84 23 57.

Weather: 08 36 68 02 74.

Snow bulletin: 08 3668 10 20.

Weather, Italian: 01 65 44 113.

Snow bulletin Italian: 01 65 31 210.

Mountain rescue: 01 65 23 82 22.

Ski lifts

"Funivi del Monte Bianco" (3462 m) : in La Palud, first turn to the left after the tunnel exit. No groomed pistes, some good off-piste, gets you back to Chamonix by the Valley Blanche. Is not included in any ski passes.

"Courmayeur Ski Lifts": a large and nice ski area.

One or several days are included in the Mont Blanc skipass.

Starting points

● "Point Helbronner" (3462 m): take the three stages of the "Funivi del Monte Bianco" cable car in "la Palud". The first village to the left after the Mont Blanc tunnel.

● Val Ferret: from the tunnel exit go left at the first bend towards La Palud. Follow the road (generally cleared) to Planpincieux, then the "cross-country ski" tracks to La Palud. Bus service between the two in winter.

● Val Veny:

a- by car: The road is not clear during the winter: information at the tourist office in Courmayeur. From the tunnel exit take the Courmayeur direction. At "la Saxe" turn right to Val Veny. Park at "la Cantine de la Visaille" or lower depending on the snow.

b- by the Courmayeur ski lifts: Take the cable car 4 km to the right after the Mont Blanc tunnel exit. Large car park. At the upper station follow the "verde" piste down to the Val Veny (the bottom chairlift station of Zerotta). From there follow the Val Veny valley.

NB: it is also possible to reach the Lac Combal via the "Arp cable car" (2755 m) by a long off piste route. Because of the steepness and the exposure of this descent, this "privilege" is reserved for people accompanied by a mountain guide or ski instructor.

61 - COL DE TOULE (3411m)
(descent)

Surprisingly few takers for this classic route!

- Map   : IGN TOP 25 3531 ET St Gervais
- Starting point : Helbronner or Aiguille du Midi cable car
- Height difference : 1250 m down, (2000 m to La Palud)
- Orientation   : south-east.
- Difficulty   : GS-A.
- Timing   : 1hr30 - 2hrs
- Time of year   : December-April
- Equipment   : as for tours on glaciers.

- Itinerary (photo 47)
From the "Pointe Helbronner" ski under the cables of the Valley Blanche téle
cabine to the "Col des Flambeaux" (3047 m). Traverse sideways to the le
under the "Grande Flambeau" to the "Col Oriental de Toule" (short climb a
the end), between the Grand Flambeau and the Aiguille de Toule.

- Descent
From the col reach the steps by a sometimes steep and icy slope (rope useful
Once on the "glacier de Toule", ski down staying mainly left. When you get t
the large flat area go to the left side of the glacier to pass the crevasses, along
side the rock ridge. Leave the glacier by the left and ski the series of small val
leys down leftwards to the "Pavillon" (2174 m), mid station of the Helbronne
cable car.

Photo 47
27b. Col d'Entrève
61. Toule glacie
62a. Brenva Glacier - 62b. left side variatio
63. "Col de Rochefor

In good snow conditions you can ski down to La Palud from "Pavillon".
Descend the slopes to the left to above the "avalanche racks" then come back
under the cables to the right. Follow the ridge for 100 m, then make a long
traverse to the left (schuss).
Ski the nice slope, scattered with larch trees, to the edge of the forest. Go
right to ski one of the couloirs (which get narrower and narrower) down to La
Palud.

- **Variation** (photo 20 and 21).
From the Aiguille de Midi follow tour n° 27 (col d'Entreves) to under the
Aiguille de Toule and then on to the "col Oriental de Toule". From when you
put your skins on, count 40 min (easy, but the terrain can be tricky).

- **Safety tips**
When the foehn (warm south wind) blows on the French side the Italian side
will generally be in fog and rain.

62 - BRENVA GLACIER

This descent, not always in condition, is on very steep slopes where finding
the route is difficult, for experts only. A fairyland setting under the
"euterey" ridge.

Map	:	IGN TOP 25 3531 ET St Gervais
Access	:	Courmayeur (or Chamonix)
Starting point	:	Helbronner cable car (or Aiguille de Midi)
Height difference	:	330 m up, 2130 m down
Orientation	:	north-east up, south-east down
Difficulty	:	VD-VGS-A
Timing	:	1hr30-2hrs up, 3-5hrs down
Time of year	:	depends on snow conditions
Equipment	:	as for tours on glaciers (50 m abseil).

Itineraries: (photos 20 and 21)
- From the Helbronner point (3462 m) follow the Valley Blanche telecabine
  cables to the "Col de la Flambeau" (3407 m). Descend to the left and pass
  under the foot of the "Aiguille de Toule" and climb south-west up the
  "Combe Maudite". Go around the "Tour Ronde" and up the small bowl to
  the left. Keep on up in the direction of the "Arête de la Brenva", then up a
  very steep slope (150 m at 50°) to reach the col (3627 m).
- From the Aiguille du Midi follow tour n° 27 to just under the "Tour Ronde".
  Then as above.

Descent: (photo 47)
From the col go down the Italian side (100m at 40°) to a snowy spine next to
the point marked 3560 m. Go left and ski down the unnamed glacier
between the south-east ridge of the "Tour Ronde" and the "Bivouac de la
Brenva". Stay mainly on the right bank of the glacier. From 2629 m, you have
two options:

a) By the right side of the Brenva glacier:

Put your skins on and cross over to the right bank of the glacier under t
"Aiguille Noire de Peuterey" (many crevasses). Continue down close to t
rocks and go around the large serac by the steadily steepening slope (ro
sometimes necessary). Reach the bottom of the glacier by skiing across
reach the moraine on the left bank under the Mont Blanc tunnel. An old ro
takes you back to the main road (15 mins walk to La Palud).

b) By the left side of the Brenva glacier (only in excellent conditions):

Ski down, following the "Rochers de la Brenva" ridge, to around 1950 m. C
carefully around the bottom of this ridge (steep, above a rock barrier) and in
a sparse forest. Abseil down a steep slopes and reach the bottom of the gl
cier by the moraine on the left bank. Then as above to La Palud.

- Variation

Tour Ronde south face (D/EGS+)

- Climb: As for the itinerary towards the Col d'Entreves, then directly belo
  the "Col Freshfield" climb up, on steeper and steeper slopes, to the south
  east ridge of the Tour Ronde. Continue up towards the summit.
- Descent: Start 100 m below the top, after the last steep section of the sno
  ridge. Down the south face towards the obvious couloir, at the bottom c
  which you traverse right (rope useful) to the south-facing slopes directl
  under the summit (350 m at 40°). This brings you back to the previous iti
  nerary.

Safety tips

These routes are only for excellent skiers familiar with mountaineering techniques.

- They are well visible from Courmayeur ski lifts. A good look is a must to judge conditions.
- The bottom of the glacier warms up quickly and becomes unskiable from the beginning of the afternoon. Start the descent early even if the snow is still hard.
- There is risk of stone fall on the right bank (Peuterey ridge).

63 - COL DE ROCHEFORT

(Aiguilles Marbrees couloir)
(circuit)

A superb descent from the "col de Rochefort", but be careful on the first lor slope (45° then 40°), especially if the snow is hard.

- Map   : IGN TOP 25 3531 ET St Gervais
- Starting point   : Helbronner cable car
- Height difference   : 100 m up, 2000 m down
- Orientation   : north then south-east
- Difficulty   : VE-VGS-A
- Timing   : 30 min up, 3-3hrs30 down
- Time of year   : depends on conditions
- Equipment   : as for tours on glaciers.

- **Itinerary** (photo 47)
  From the bottom of the Helbronner steps schuss north-east, across the "Co du Geant" bowl to the north-east foot of the "Petite Aiguille Marbree". Clim up, skis on sack, towards the "Col de Rochefort" and join the ridge on the right close to the rocks).

- **Descent**
  Traverse to the right, under the summit, and into the couloir (200m at 45°) by crossing between the rocks. Once onto the glacier, the slope shallows out Two options: continue down the right side of the glacier, near to the rocks After the steeper passage which gets you off the glacier, go left to come under the seracs. At 2450 m traverse imperatively left (long) to the slopes under the south side of the "Aiguille Rouge de Rochefort", and down to the valley.
  Or second option (recommended): go across to the left bank. Ski down several slopes to leave the glacier. Reach the route previously descript.

- **Safety tips**
  You can use a rope at the top of the couloir, belaying off the rocks. From the end of February start down before 10 am.

64 - MONT BLANC BY THE AIGUILLES GRISES
(return trip)

Himalayan atmosphere and a very commiting exceptional setting, make this the best way up to the top of Europe.

Map	: IGN TOP 25 3531 ET St Gervais
Starting point	: 1) Cantine de la Visaille,
	2) The Courmayeur lifts in winter
Height difference	: Day 1) 1410 m
	Day 2) 1740 m
Orientation	: south-east then north-west for the summit ridge
Difficulty	: VD-VGS-A
Timing	: Day 1) 5-7hrs up; Day 2) 6-8hrs up
Time of year	: May-June
Equipment	: as for tours on glaciers.

Itinerary (photos 48, 49 and 51).
- **Day1**: From the Cantine de la Visaille (or higher) follow the road to the "Lac de Combal". Climb the moraine (on foot) by a steep path, then get onto the right bank of the "Miage" glacier.
With good snow cover it is possible to climb a couloir on skis between the moraine and the base of the "Mont Suc" to reach the same point.
- Climb the glacier, then either:
a) poor snow cover: go past the end of the "Glacier du Dome" and at around 2650 m come over to the left bank of the glacier and leave it by a climbing traverse to the right. Then follow the summer route traversing a steep slope to reach a spur under the hut. Follow this spur (cables) to reach the hut. The first building is the winter hut.
b) good snow cover: climb up the centre of the glacier weaving between the crevasses to where, around 2700 m, it becomes less steep. Leave left and climb the spur (cables) beneath the refuge. If the snow permits, you can also come up the left side of the spur (steep) to the refuge.
- **Day 2:** From the refuge traverse horizontally (on foot) the ridge and descend onto the "Dome Glacier". Climb it as best you can (steep and crevassed)

first by the left, then by the middle towards the south-east spur of the "Tour des Aiguilles Grises", then up across to the spur coming off the point marked 3731 m. Climb this branch of the "glacier du Dome" on the right. As the slope becomes less steep, come over to the left and up the slope leading to the Aiguilles Grises ridge well to the right of the "Col des Aiguilles Grises". Follow this ridge to the "Dome du Gouter" (tricky). Under the Dome traverse sideways to the "Col du Dome" and the Vallot hut. The summit is up the "Arête des Bosses".

- **Descent** (photo 51)
Same way to start with, then from the "Piton des Italiens" follow to the right the delicate, corniced ridge which descends to the "Col de Bionassay". On to the Italian Bionassay Glacier by a steep slope, then down its right bank to the top of the Miage Glacier where you rejoin the route up.

- **Variation**
An original route from Les Contamines, is to get to the Mont Blanc by the Elisabetta refuge via the Robert Blanc hut (Tour 13).

Photo 48
64. Mont Blanc by the Aiguilles Grises route
65. Elisabetta Soldini hut
66. "Petit Mont Blanc" - 66a. "Aiguille Orientale de Tré-la-Tête"
67a and 67b. "Col de Tré-la-Tête"
68. "Dôme de neige de l'Aiguille des Glaciers" - 69. "Col de la Seigne"

- Safety tips
  - If you go to the hut by the "glacier du Dome", rope up! (crevasses).
  - When you get to the refuge, walk up the beginning of the route to the Dome. These tracks, frozen in the night, make the traverse easier in the morning.
  - Observe the descent route on the Italien side of the "Miage" glacier from the Aiguille Grises ridge. It is complex, especially when the snow cover poor.

Photo 49

64. descent route - 64a. Gonella hut by the summer pat!
64b. Gonella hut by the "Glacier du Dome

Photo 50: 69. Col de la Seigne - 69a. Pointe Léchaud

Col de La Seigne

69

Pointe Léchaud

69a

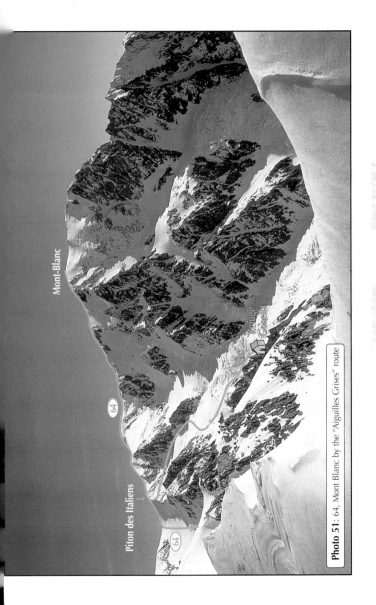

Photo 51: 64, Mont Blanc by the "Aiguilles Grises" route

Mont-Blanc

Piton des Italiens

64

64

65 - ELISABETTA SOLDINI HUT (2200m)
(hut access)

At the bottom of the "Val Veny", this refuge makes a good base camp f
some little known routes, in one of the wildest parts of these mountair
The winter refuge is not very nice. Bring a warm bag, the blankets are ofte
damp. There is no gas.

- Map   : IGN TOP 25 3531 ET St Gervais
- Starting point   : a) Cantine de la Visaille
                         b) Courmayeur lifts
- Height difference   : a) 540 m up; b) 630 m down, 200 m up
- Orientation   : a) north-east; b) north then north-east
- Difficulty   : a) VE-IMS - b) VE-GS
- Timing   : a) 2 - 2hrs30; b) 1hr30 - 2hrs
- Time of year   : 1) April-June; 2) January-April.

- **Itineries** photos 48
  a) From the Cantine follow the road towards the Lac Combal. Cross a bridg
  and continue up the road, past some ruins, and to the refuge just above (a
  the base of the north-east ridge of the "Pyramides Calcaires").
  b) by the Courmayeurs lifts. See page 175.

- **Descent** By itinerary a).

- **Safety tip**
  The descent from the Arp cable car should only be done when the snowpack
  is stable.

66 - PETIT MONT BLANC (3424m)
(circuit)

This route, little used, in an extraordinary glacial setting, is reserved only for the experienced.

Map	: IGN TOP 25 3531 ET St Gervais
Starting point	: Refuge Elisabetta
Height difference	: 1425 m up and down
Orientation	: south-east up. South south-east for the descent
Difficulty	: VD-VGS-A
Timing	: 5-6hrs up
Time of year	: March-May
Equipment	: as for tours on glaciers.

Itinerary (photo 48 and 52)

From the refuge go down to the "Lac Combal" and take the path that starts under the right moraine of the Italian side of "glacier de Miage" (point marked 1958 m). Traverse up to the left (steep, south-east facing slopes) towards the obvious couloir between the "Aiguille de Combal" and the "Mont Suc". Climb up and past the refuge "Petit Mont Blanc" (on the left, 3047m, 9 places). Up the wide ridge to the top.

Descent

Come down a few metres, and drop down a steep couloir (rope useful) onto the Petit Mont Blanc Glacier. Down its right bank (crevasses) to the "Glacier de la Lée Blanche", where it flattens out (around 2850 m). From here:
- either come down the glacier's left bank and traverse it at 2500 m to reach its right bank then get off it as best you can (crevasses, seracs). Work right, over a moraine, and back down to the refuge on wide slopes (see route 67).
- Or, preferably, traverse the flat area at 2850 m to a steep couloir between the right side of the glacier and the northern extremity of the buttress coming down from the "Aiguille d'Estelette". Ski down it (150m at 40°), then as above, back to the refuge.

- **Variation**:

  After the short descent onto the "Petit Mont Blanc" glacier, you can climb on skis to the foot of the north-east ridge of the "Aiguille Oriental de Tre-la-Tête" Get to the summit on foot (40-45°, VD-VGS-A).

- **Safety tips**:

  Optimal conditions, which means no snow on the bottom of the path, but enough on the glacier (well visible from the refuge), are rare...
  You could cut the climb up with a night at the "bivouac Petit Mont Blanc".
  Note: the terminal tongue of the "glacier de Lee Blanche" is impassable.

Photo 52

66. "Petit Mont Blanc
66a. Toward "Aiguille Orientale de Tré-la-Tête

Petit Mont-Blanc

Bivouac
du Petit Mont-Blanc

66

66

66b

Howard Hindley 67

67 - "COL DE TRE LA TETE" (3515)
(return)

M agnificent, serious route, little used.

- Map : IGN TOP 25 3531 ET St Gervais
- Starting point : Refuge Elisabetta
- Height difference : 1315 m
- Orientation : south-east
- Difficulty : D-VGS-A
- Timing : 5-6hrs up, 2-3hrs down
- Time of year : March-June
- Equipment : as for tours on glaciers.

- **Itinerary** (photo 48)
  From the refuge go up the valleyed slopes to the north-west, towards the roc
  buttresses of the "Aiguille d'Estelette". After traversing a moraine near 240
  m, two routes are possible to the "Lée Blanche" glacier.

  a) (recommended) Alongside the buttress to a snowy couloir, which separa
  tes it from the right side of the glacier. Up this to a flatter area. At abou
  2850 m come back left, towards the "Aiguille d'Estelette" and follow the
  right bank of the glacier, by an arc, to the east ridge of the "Aiguille de l
  Lée Blanche". This cuts the top part of the glacier in two.
  Get over the ridge by a steep snow couloir to the right of the point marke
  3300 m. Cross the huge glacial cirque to easily reach the "Col de Tré-la
  Tête".

  b) Around 2500 m get onto the glacier as best you can, traverse over to its
  left bank and climb up it. Pass under the "Glacier du Petit Mont Blanc" to
  the flatter area at about 2850 m. From here climb the left bank of the gla
  cier (steep, crevassed) to the glacial cirque, and the col.

Descent

By route **a** (recommended). Route **b** is more complex.

Variation:

You can also reach the summit of the "Aiguille Nord de Tré-la-Tête", by traversing, on the Tre-la-Tête side, the west face suspended glacier (see variation of itinerary 19).

Safety tips

The "Lée Blanche" glacier faces south-east. Leave early if you want skiable snow for the descent.

68 - "DOME DE NEIGE DES GLACIERS" (3592m)
(return trip)

A super route, from all points of view.

- Map   : IGN TOP 25 3531 ET St Gervais
- Starting point   : Refuge Elisabetta
- Height difference : 1390 m
- Orientation   : east then south
- Difficulty   : D-GS-A
- Timing   : 5-6hrs
- Time of year   : March-June
- Equipment   : as for tours on glaciers.

- **Itinerary** (photos 13 and 48)
From the refuge climb the small valley between an obvious moraine and th
"Pyramides Calcaires". Around 2550 m you reach a col. Traverse some ver
steep slopes and, on the right, climb up to the small col to the right of th
"Montagne des Glaciers" (2747 m, steep at the end). From this col travers
down on the right a few metres then back up, still rightwards, to the obviou
passage of the south-west ridge of the "Petite Aiguille des Glaciers" (betwee
the points marked 3102 m and 3000 m). Climb the "Glacier des Glaciers"
alongside the ridge (steep). At 3250 m traverse left and follow the glacial val
ley, which takes you easily up to the "Dome de Neige des Glaciers". You ca
carry on up on skis to around 3700 m (the foot of the Aiguille des Glaciers)

- **Descent:** Same way down.

- **Variation**
You can come down the French side by the "Pentes des Cabottes" to the
"Chalets des Mottets" (tour no 14a) then back into Italy by the "Col de la
Seigne".

69 - COL DE LA SEIGNE (2516m)
(return trip)

Traditional passage between Italy and France. The famous "Tour de Mont Blanc" goes through here, but it's deserted in winter.

Map	:	IGN TOP 25 3531 ET St Gervais
Starting point	:	Refuge Elisabetta.
Height difference	:	370m up
Orientation	:	north-east
Difficulty	:	E-IMS
Timing	:	1 - 2hrs
Time of year	:	March-May
Equipment	:	as for tours on glaciers.

Itinerary: (photo 48 and 50)
From the refuge go down 50m to the "Lée Blanche" valley, climb its left bank, and then some large ,wide, slopes to the col (enormous cairn).

Descent: Same way down.

Variation
You could go over the col to the French side and the Chalets des Mottets (GS), or climb the "Pointe Lechaud" by the "Col de Chavannes" (D-GS). Very nice view.

70 - COL DE MALATRA (2928m)
(return trip)

The biggest interest of this route is to give you a good view over the Itali.
side of the Mont Blanc.

- Map : IGN 3630 OT Chamonix. Suisse 1365 Grand St Berna.
- Starting point : Val Ferret
- Height difference : 1370 m
- Orientation : north-west then south-west
- Difficulty : E+ -IMS
- Timing : 5-6hrs up, 1hr30-2hrs30 down
- Time of year : December-April.

- **Itinerary** (photos 53 and 54)
Follow the cross-country ski tracks to the "Chalets de la Vachy" (restaurant
Continue on the tracks to the second sharp bend, then leave them by the righ
and climb up some steep slopes through the forest, staying mainly left (pat
at the beginning). You come out of the forest onto less steep slopes which tak.
you up to the new Bonatti refuge (not marked on the map). Follow a larg.
shelf to around 2450 m where you come up against some sustained slope:
Climb up these on the left to the "Combe du Col de Malatra". Carry on up
on the left, over some steeper parts, then traverse over to the col (between
two rock shoulders).

- **Descent**: Same way down.

- **Variation**:
From the shelf (2300 m) you can climb up right towards "Pas" or the "Tête
d'Entre-deux-Sauts", not as long, and you can make a circuit by going down
the other side.

→
Photo 53
70. "col de Malatra" (lower part

The AIGUILLES ROUGES

These mountains are mostly inclued in a nature reserve and offer a magnifice
playground for ski touring with the Mont Blanc as a backdrop.
The Brevent and Flegere lift systems make certain routes easily accessible. T
north facing Bérard valley often benefits from excellent snow conditions

Lodgings

"Gites d'etape" at Vallorcine.

- Chalet Mermoud, 04 50 54 60 03 (le Morzay).

- Chalet Saint Louis, 04 50 54 61 37 (le Plan Droit).

- Chalet Skiroc, 04 50 54 60 32 (le Buet).

Useful addresses

- Vallorcine tourist office, 04 50 54 60 71

- Vallorcine train station, 04 50 54 60 28

- Vallorcine Guides office, 04 50 5460 69

- Ski lifts, see Chamonix and Argentière sections.

Starting points

1) Col des Montets: from Chamonix, direction Switzerland, past Argentière
   Park opposite the nature reserve chalet.

2) Le Buet: the first little village after the "col des Montets". Carpark and train
   station opposite the hotel du Buet.

3) Le Couteray: After the Buet cross the bridge and take the small road to the
   left.

4) Flégère cable car: From Chamonix, direction Argentière, at Les Praz, jus
   after the roundabout. Take the cable car then the chairlift of the Index.

5) Telesieige du Col Cornu: Part of the Brevent ski resort, from Planpraz (mid
   station) take the Altitude 2000 chairlift and ski down the Combe de Vioz.

6) Le Plateau d'Assy: From Chamonix descend towards Sallanches, then take
   the road to the "Plateau d'Assy", then on to the "Plaine Joux" ski resort.

71 - COL DE BERARD (2460m)
(return trip)

The Bérard Valley, loved by ski tourers, keeps its isolated, savage character. The climb up is becoming a classic.

Map	: IGN 3630 OT Chamonix
Starting point	: Le Buet
Height difference	: 1130 m
Orientation	: north-east
Difficulty	: SD-BS
Timing	: 4-4hrs30 up, 1-2hrs down
Time of year	: December-May.

Itinerary: (photo 55 and 62)
From the carpark follow the babylift piste towards the old houses of La Poya. To the right, climb a steep hill through the forest to the "cascade de Bérard" (30m waterfall, restaurant, open June to September). Climb up the right bank of the stream (sometimes icy) and cross it by the "Pont de la Vordette", then up its left bank by a steep, narrow path. A long flat passage takes you up to the "Pierre à Bérard" refuge (Generally buried under the snow). Go up the "Combe de Bérard" on sustained slopes to the col.

- Descent
Same way down but stay always on the right bank after the long flat section (1750 m).

- Variation (photo 56)
You can also climb up west, above the Pierre à Bérard hut, to reach the Col du Cochon (not marked on the French IGN maps; marked at 2497 m on the Swiss CN maps). It is situated on the ridge between the Aiguille de Bérard and the Col de Salenton.

- Safety tips

Depending on the conditions the bottom part of the valley sometimes look like a rally cross rather than a nice forest ski, narrow passages, blocks, stee traverses, trees, etc... Ski well in control.

→

Photo 55:

71. "Col de Bérard - 72. towards "Mont Buet"
75. "Crochues-Bérard" Descent - 75a. "Breche de l'Aiguille de Bérard"
80. Descent from the "col du Lac Cornu" via "col de Bérard"

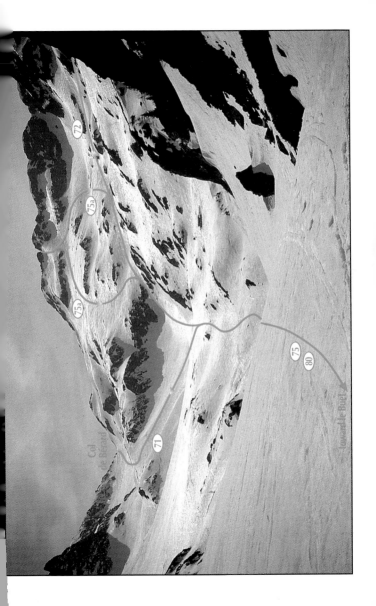

72 - "LE MONT BUET" (3096m)
(return trip)

Called the Ladies Mont Blanc this is a classic but long route with an exceptional view over all the northern Alps.

- Map : IGN TOP 25 3630 OT Chamonix
- Starting point : Le Buet
- Height difference : 1780 m up and down
- Orientation : north-west, then south-east
- Difficulty : SD-GS
- Timing : 6-7hrs up, 2-3hrs down
- Time of year : December-June

- **Itinerary** (photos 55 and 56)
  As for tour n° 71 to the "Pierre a Bérard". From there climb north-west to the "Col de Salenton". Traverse right, under the "Aiguille de Salenton", the climb left to a small col. Continue crossing up on a vague shoulder and the follow the large ridge "La Mortine" to the summit.

- **Descent**: Same way down (30° in places).

- **Variation**:
  You can ski directly down the south-east face, avoiding the rock barriers, to the "Creux aux Vaches". This forms a bowl, then a narrow couloir which you leave by the right to get back to the "Pierre à Bérard" (several passages at 35°, notably near the top, VGS).

Safety tips
This is a long route and with its S-E orientation you must leave early to avoid avalanches, particularly on the S-E face and under the "Aiguille de Salenton".

→
Photo 56
71a. "co du Cochon" - 72. Mont Buet - 72a. "Creux aux Vaches"

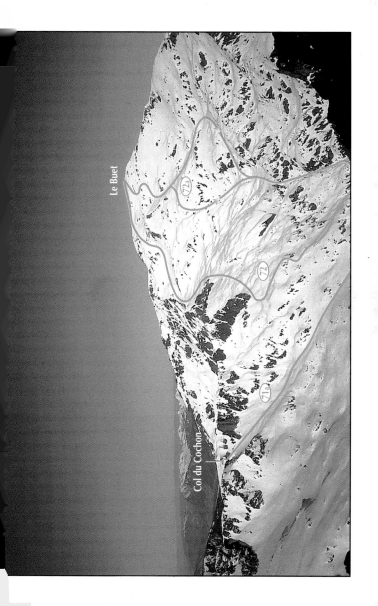

73 - COL DE LA TERRASSE (2648m)
(return trip)

Part of the Perrons chain, border between France and Switzerland, busy summer, very quiet in winter.

- Map : IGN TOP 25 3630 OT Chamonix
  Swiss map: 1324 Barberine and 1344 Col de Balme.
- Starting point : Le Couteray
- Height difference : 1300m
- Orientation : south-east, then east
- Difficulty : D-GS
- Timing : 4-5hrs up, 2hrs down
- Time of year : December-April
- Equipment : crampons useful.

- **Itinerary** (photo 57)
  From "Couteray" take the forest trail up to the "Chalets de Loriaz". When the trail leaves the forest go north over a large flat section passing the chalets on their left. The slope then steepens and forms a wide cirque to the left. Climb to the left to come up against the last slope and steep couloir which takes you up to the col between the "Aiguille de Charmoz" and the "Pointe de la Terrasse"

- **Descent**: Same way down.

- **Variations**:
  - *by the Veudale gorge* -GS- From the col descend north facing gentle slopes to a shelf (2700 m). Ski down to the right a steeper slope to go into the Veudale gorge, then down to the road above the Emosson lake. Traverse the dam and follow the road to "Finhaut", where you take the train back to Le Buet.
  - *"Pointe de la Terrasse" north face*: You can also, from the col, follow the north ridge to the "Pointe de la Terrasse" and ski down the north face (150m at 45°, VGS) to rejoin the route up.
  - *by Loriaz* : you can go down one of the couloirs which cut through the forest, notably the one under the electric cables (Watch out - these routes are all avalanche prone).

Photo 57

73. "Col de la Terrasse" - 73a. Towards Veudales Gorge

74 - COL DE L'ENCRENAZ (2579m)
(return trip)

Less frequented than the routes around it, but the first slopes are fairly trick

- Map   : IGN TOP 25 3630 OT Chamonix
                          or Swiss map 1344 Col de Balme
- Starting point   : Col des Montets
- Height difference   : 1150m
- Orientation   : mostly east but one section north
- Difficulty   : D-GS
- Timing   : 3-4hrs up, 1-1hr30 down
- Time of year   : January-April.

- **Itinerary** (photo 58)
From 500 m after the "col des Montets" (Vallorcine side) climb up the wid
deforested slopes (west) to the left. At about 1550 m look for the three steep
narrow, couloirs to the left: take the left hand one (rock barrier to its left
Climb it on the right, on a sort of shoulder, then, when it widens, up th
middle. Around 1850 m you come out onto a crest, which you climb up righ
towards the "Aiguille de Praz Torrent". At about 2000 m traverse the stee
slope to the left, at the base of the north-east ridge of the "Aiguille d
Mesure".
Up the steep slopes next to this ridge, then traverse over to the "Combe d
l'Encrenaz", which you follow up to the col (steep at the end, stay right).

- **Descent**: Same way down (passage at 40°).

- **Variation**
Descent to the Bérard Valley (VGS). Go down the north-west face, directly
under the "Aiguille Morris", via a small valley, then by wide steep slopes. A
around 2300 m go right and weave between the rocks (exposed) down to the
Berard valley, then down its right side to Le Buet. Only possible when the
snow cover is good.

Photo 58

74. "Col de l'Encrenaz" - 76 a. "Beugeant- Encrenaz": descent rout

Col
de l'Encrenaz

Aiguille de Mesure

74

76a

↓ Col des Montets

75 - THE CROCHUES - BERARD TRAVERSE (2701m)

A magnificent easily accessible route on three sides of the Aiguilles Rouge. The snow conditions in the traverse between the two cols is often trick (ice, avalanche debris).

- Map   : IGN TOP 25 3630 OT Chamonix,
                         or Suisse 1344 Col de Balme
- Starting point   : Flegere cable car
- Height difference   : 500 m up, 1430m down
- Orientation   : East then south south-west, then north-east
- Difficulty   : SD+-GS
- Timing   : 4hrs30-5hrs30
- Time of year   : December-April
- Equipment   : 50 m rope.

- **Itinerary** (photos 59, 60 and 64)
  From the top of the "Index" chairlift (2385 m) go down a few metres to th north into a large bowl. Skins on, then traverse up to the north and pass t the right of a rock buttress (point marked 2578 m). Continue on and up steep slope to a vague ridge. Continue traversing left to come under the "Co de Crochues". This col (2701 m), used in winter, is to the left of the one use in summer (2704 m). Climb up the final slope to the col (steeper and steeper on foot, 1hr).
  From here go down a few metres to the right, then, without losing too muc height, make a wide turn sideways above the "Combe de la Balme" to come up against the rock buttresses of the west ridge of the "Aiguille du Belvedère". Go around its base and climb up, to the right, the "Combe d'Envers de Berard" to the "Col de Bérard" (40 min up, between the "Aiguille de Bérard" and the "Pointe Alphonse Favre).

Photo 59

75. Col des Crochue
76. 77. 78. Towards "lac Blanc" - 79a. "Aiguille de la Glière" desce.

- **Descent**: (photo 55 and 62). Descend the wide Bérard bowl which leads the "Vallon de Bérard". Go down its right side and, at around 1500 m, follc the right bank of the river (some parts are steep and there is a risk of falli into the river, particulary if the snow is hard). You'll soon reach the "casca(de Bérard" cabin from where a forest track leads you to the Poya ski runs a le Buet village. You can take the train from here back to Les Praz.

- **Variations** (photos 55, 60 and 62)
  The "Breche de l'Aiguille de Berard", (2663 m, GS): From the "Bérard" bo\ (after the long sideways traverse) cross to the north-west towards the stee couloir which takes you to the ridge line joining the "Petite" and the "Granc Aiguille de Berard". Follow it to the "Brêche" (notch). On the other side s down the wide slopes of the "Combe de Berard" (sustained at first).
  The "Glacier du Mort" (2700 m, VGS+-A): halfway between the two col climb up the couloir on foot, under the "Pointe Alphonse Favre (200 m Once on the ridge keep climbing towards the Aiguille de Belvedère (mixec 2/3 French grade) to a fore summit not marked on the map. From there descend, working right on 40° slopes, to the little glacier, then down to th Berard Valley.

- **Safety tips**
  The climb up to the col des Crochues is steep and often on hard snow. Don' hesitate to rope up for the last 100 m.
  - Wait until the snow softens to make the traverse between the two cols.

Photo 6(

75. Crochues - Bérard traverse- 75a. "Brêche de l'aiguille de Bérarc
75b. Towards the "glacier du Mort" - 80. "col du lac Cornu" - "col de Bérard" travers

76 - "COL DE BEUGEANT" (2807m)
(traverse)

After a small technical passage on the way up, the descent is a real pleas~
re, either on powder in the "Vallon de Bérard" or, if you time it right, ~
good spring snow in the combe de l'Encrenaz.

- Map   : IGN TOP 25 3630 OT Chamonix,
                     or Suisse 1344 Col de Balme
- Starting point : Flégère cable car
- Height difference : 700 m up, 1700m down
- Orientation   : south, south-west up, then either, north-west (Bérard)
                     or east (Encrenaz) down
- Difficulty   : D-GS-A
- Timing   : 2-3hrs up, 1hr30 - 2hrs30 down
- Time of year   : December-May
- Equipment   : as for tours on glaciers + 4 extra carabiners.

- **Itinerary** (photo 59, 61 and 64).
From the top of the "Index" chair lift leave right, towards the north-east, an~
make a long sideways traverse, cutting across several small valleys. Try not t~
lose too much height.
Get to the top of the "Combe des Crochues", which has, on its left, the south~
east ridge of the "Aiguilles Crochues". Ski down it, then, on the left, after ~
shelf, traverse a steep and exposed slope (the base of the ridge). Skins on,
then traverse up north-east to the "Lac Blanc" refuge (steep path).
- *If snow conditions are not safe* (ice, wind slab) go further down the bowl t~
a shelf under the base of the ridge, around 2100 m. You will see the top o~
the "Chavannes" telesiege. Climb up a small bowl to the left, then follow the
series of small bowls up to the refuge (closed in winter).
Pass under the refuge and climb up, to the right of the lake, a succession o~
bumps to a bowl, which you go around to the left.

Photo 61
76. "col de Beugeant

Col
de Beugeant

toward Lac Blanc

Up some steep slopes to the north, which narrow down at around 2780 m. Put your skis on your sack, rope up, and follow a tricky, vague ledge (pitons often snow covered, climbing sideways to the left of a rock barrier. One last steep slope leads up to the col (crampons).

- **Descents** (photo 58 and 62).
  a) By the Col d'Encrenaz: from the col (slings to the right), after a steep wall (50 m at 40°), you arrive at a flat area below a rounded bump. Traverse right towards the "col d'Encrenaz" (tour n° 74), cross the col and follow the "Combe d'Encrenaz". At about 2250 m go left and pass the foot of the east ridge of the "Aiguille de Mesure" to arrive in the "Vallon de Praz Torrent". Descend the wide slopes on a shoulder and, near 1850 m, drop down left into a steep couloir (40°). Near the bottom, leave it by the left, then ski down easier slopes to rejoin, to the right, the road to the col des Montets (train back to the "Praz de Chamonix" from "Le Buet" station 1km).

→

Photo 62:
71. Towards "col de Bérard"
75. "Crochues-Bérard" descent - 75b. "Pointe Adolphe Favre" and "glacier du Mort descent"
76a. "Beugeant - Encrenaz descent"
76b. "Beugeant - vallon de Bérard"
77. "col du Belvédère" descent

b) By the Bérard Valley: from the flat area traverse left to a small col (250 m) on the ridge separating the "glacier de Beugeant" from the "glacier d'Anneuley". Drop down the other side of this col and down sustained slopes. At the bottom, avoid the rock barriers by traversing left to join the Bérard valley at about 1900 m. Then follow route n° 71 back to Le Buet.

- Safety tips
Some years you can find crevasses on the "glacier de Beugeant" if the snow cover is poor.

→
Photo 63:
77. "col du Belvédère"
78. "col des Dards"

Aiguille
du Belvédère

Tourard
La Flégère

77

78

77 - "COL DU BELVEDERE" (2780m)
(traverse)

An easy climb followed by a very serious descent, which begins in a steep narrow gully. There are not many skiers who would attempt a turn... than you rope!

- Map   : IGN TOP 25 3630 OT Chamonix
- Starting point   : Flégère cable car
- Height difference   : 680 m up, 1600m down
- Orientation   : south-east up, north-west down
- Difficulty   : E-VGS-A
- Timing   : 4-5hrs in total
- Time of year   : December-May
- Equipment   : as for tours on glaciers, 100 m of rope

- **Itinerary** (photos 59, 63 and 64)
  As for n° 76 to the "Lac Blanc". Opposite the refuge climb north-west up the Vallon "de Belvedère". Wide gentle slopes lead up to the col (to the right of the "Aiguille de Belvedere").

- **Descent** (photo 62)
  Descend the steep, narrow, north-west gully (150m at 45°, slings to the right, a rope is useful for the first 50 m), down onto the "glacier de Berard". Descend by either side to avoid the crevasses in the middle, then down the sustained slopes (30°-35°) to arrive at the top of the Berard Valley and as for tour n° 71 to "Le Buet".

→

Photo 64:
75. "col des Crochues" - 76. "col de Beugeant"
77. "col du Belvédère" - 78. "col des Dards"
79. "Col de la Glière" descent - 79b. "Col des Lacs Noirs" descent

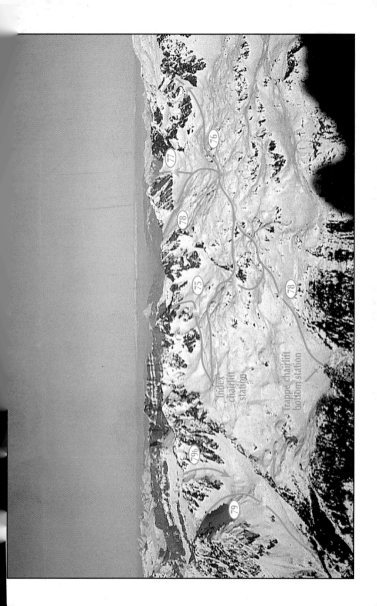

- Variation

By the way up (GS): Near 2100 m, where you put your skins on, continue c wide slopes, always towards the right. Rejoin the piste "La Trappe", and tl chairlift of the same name back to La Flégère (some money for the lift).

- Safety tips

With poor snowcover crevasses can appear on the Bérard glacier.

→
Photo 65:
79. "col de la Glière" descent
79b. "col des lacs Noirs" descent

Col de la
Glière

79b

79

toward Flégère lift

78 - "COL DES DARDS" (2790m)
(return trip)

A nice way to learn ski touring.

- Map : IGN TOP 25 3630 OT Chamonix, or 3530 Samoens
- Starting point : Flegere cable car
- Height difference : 700 m up, 1330m down
- Orientation : south-east then north-east
- Difficulty : E-IMS
- Timing : 2-3hrs up, 1-1hr30 down
- Time of year : December-April

- **Itinerary** (photos 59, 63 and 64)
  Follow routes n° 76 and 77 to the "Vallon de Belvedère" then, arour
  2500 m, come back left on wide slopes to the "Col des Dards".

- **Descent** (photo 62)
  Same way down to about 2100 m, then continue on wide slopes, alway
  towards the right, to the piste and chairlift of the "Trappe" and back to L
  Flégère (some money for the lift).

- **Variation**
  The north couloir of the "Aiguille Nord des Crochues", SD-VGS-A: From th
  "col des Dards" you can climb the "pointe Nord des Aiguilles Crochues
  then, by following the ridge towards the south-west, get to this short, ver
  steep couloir, which descends on the right towards the "Combe de Balme"
  Continue by tour n° 75 Crochues-Berard.

78 bis - "COL DE LA FLORIA" (2752m)
(traverse)

This route demands a fine appreciation of the risks involved in this sport, with a cornice to cross and frequent wind slab. As is often the case for this be of route, good conditions are rare.

Map   : IGN TOP 25 3630 OT Chamonix or 3530 ET Samoens
Starting point   : Teleseige de l'Index
Height difference : 900 m up, 1900m down
Orientation   : south-east up, north-west down
Difficulty   : D-VGS-A
Timing   : 1hr30 up
Time of year   : February-March
Equipment   : as for tours on glaciers.

Itinerary
From the top of the Index climb north-west to the base of a well visible couloir next to which rises the "Gendarme Wehrlin". Climb this couloir to where the slope gentles out, then work over to the right to the col.

Descent
From the col, start down the top of the "glacier de la Floria" (100m at 45°). With the constant risk of wind slab on this slope, rope up the first skier. Once on the glacier join, in obvious fashion, the "combe de Balme" and ski down it to a large shelf, scattered with rocks, at around 1950 m. From here climb the "combe de l'Envers de Bérard" and tour n° 75.

Aiguille
de la Glière

Photo 66: 79a. "Aiguille de la Glière"
80. Towards "Combe du Pouce"

Aiguille de la Charlanon

Col du
Lac Cornu

80
79

80
79

Photo 67: 79. "col du lac Cornu-Col de la Glière" traverse
80. " Col du lac Cornu- Col de Berard" traverse

79 - "COL DU LAC CORNU" (2414m) - "COL DE LA GLIERE" (2461r
(traverse)

A nice little tour between two resorts, which now have a cable car betwee
their mid-stations.

- Map : IGN TOP 25 3630 OT Chamonix, or 3530 ET Samoen
- Access : The Brevent ski resort
- Starting point : Télésiège du Col Cornu
- Height difference : 200 m up, 800 m down
- Orientation : west then east
- Difficulty : E-GS
- Timing : 1hr30-2hrs in total
- Time of year : December-May.

- **Itinerary** (photo 67).
  From the top of the "col Cornu"chairlift, go a few metres down the red pist
  "La Charlanon" to the rescue hut. Climb up, on foot, the steep slope opposi
  te, which brings you up onto a vague ridge. Follow this towards the right to
  the "Col du Lac Cornu". From here descend diagonally to the right, on a wes
  facing slope, to a large shelf at around 2350 m. Climb up, on the right, to the
  "Col de la Glière".
  If there is no avalanche risk you can traverse directly between the two col
  on skis.

- **Descent** (photos 64 and 65)
  From the col descend, on the left (Chamonix side), a steep couloir between
  some rock barriers. You enter into the "combe de la Glière", which you follow easily to where it steepens, and then you join to the left the piste of the
  "combe Lachenal".
  Just before the departure point of the chairlift "des Evettes", a cable car takes
  you back to the Brevent resort.

Variation (photos 59,66)

- The "Aiguille de la Glière" (2852 m): from the "col de la Glière" stay on the west face and follow a system of gullies towards the north. You arrive in a large cirque. Climb it in the direction of the "Aiguille de la Glière". The slope steepens. Cross right to get over the rock barrier and onto the south-east ridge, which you follow to the summit.

Descent

By the east face and the "Gendarme Wehrlin" couloir to the Index chailift and pistes (VGS).

- It is equally possible, and very interesting, to descend the "combe de La Glière" from the "col des Lacs Noirs" (VGS - photos 64 and 65).

If it is not too late you can lengthen the tour by doing the Crochues-Berard traverse (tour n° 75).

80 - "COL DU LAC CORNU" - "COL DE BERARD"
by the "combe du Pouce"
(traverse)

A nice outing which is becoming popular.

- Map   : IGN TOP 25 3630 OT Chamonix, or 3530 ET Samoen
- Access   : Chamonix
- Starting point : "Col Cornu" chairlift
- Height difference : 900 m up, 1950 m down
- Orientation   : west, then south-west, then north-west
- Difficulty   : E-VGS
- Timing   : 4-6hrs
- Time of year   : February-April

- **Itinerary** (photos 55, 50, 55 and 67)
  Follow tour n° 79 to the "col de la Glière". From here follow a series of small valleys to the north, which bring you out into a wide cirque. To the left under the point marked 2685 m, descend alongside an obvious ridge and into a small gully. Ski the wide steep slopes to the right, into the "combe de la Pouce", and carry on down it to about 2250 m (this bowl terminates further down by a rock barrier). Cross to the right, without losing height (tricky and exposed), and over the hillock separating the "combe du Pouce" (not named on the map), from the "combe de la Balme", under the point marked 2271 m. Continue down, working slightly right, until you see a ramp overlooked by a small cliff. Descend this ramp diagonally to the right to come out into the "combe de la Balme" near the point marked 1937 m. Traverse the bottom of this bowl, then climb towards the "col de Bérard" (rejoin tour n° 75).

- **Safety tips**
  If snow conditions are not good enough to traverse to the point marked 2271 m, it is possible to get down the rock barrier on its far left side using steep couloirs (rope useful), then climbing back up obliquely right to the point marked 2143 m, where you rejoin the route.

81 - "AIGUILLETTE DES HOUCHES" (2285m)
(traverse)

This varied route, not too high, alternates gentle climbs and sustained slopes. Better to do when the snow cover goes right down to the valley floor.

Map   : IGN TOP 25 3531 ET St Gervais or 3530 ET Samoens
Starting point   : Brevent cable car
Height difference : 200 m up for 1350 m down
Orientation   : north, then south.
Difficulty   : E-GS
Timing   : 2-4hrs in total
Time of year   : December-March

Itinerary (photo 68)
From the top of the cable car go a few metres down the piste, then come back to the left, and on sustained slopes cut up by rock barriers, go down to the "Lac du Brevent". Underneath the lake you come out onto the huge slopes which dominate the "Torrent de la Diosaz". Climb up the slope on the left, cut up by many small rock barriers, in the direction of the "col de Bel Lachat" (2130 m). Just before the col, attack the wide slopes to the right which lead up to the "Aiguillette des Houches". Reach the summit by a snow ridge.

- **Descent** (photo 69)
Down a short, steep slope, south, (Les Houches side). Continue by crossing left on easier slopes. At about 1950 m cross right, over a vague rise, onto the south-west facing slopes of the "Plan de Benoi". Down into, and through the forest (clearings, paths) towards the "Hameau du Plan de la Cry". Then on to the "Hameau du Bettey" or the "Hameau de Coupeau", where you could have left your car, or the train station, situated below.

- **Variation**
From the top, after the short, steep slope, cross right to ski down the sustained couloirs in the forest. You arrive, after battling through, at the "Hameau du Plan de la Cry".

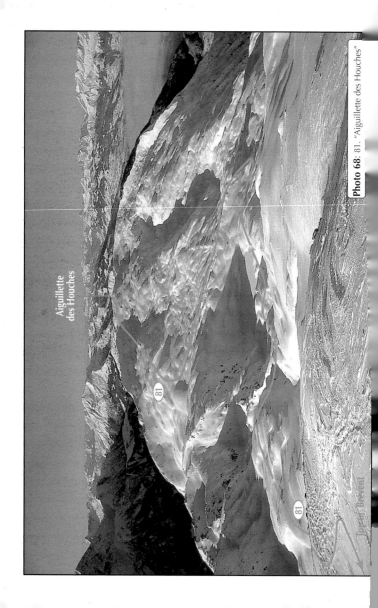

Aiguillette
des Houches

Photo 68 : 81. "Aiguillette des Houches"

Aiguillette
des Houches
↓

81

81a

Plan de la Cry

à l'Aiaui

Photo 69: 81. "Aiguillette des Houches descent-81a. Variation

82 - "POINTE NOIRE DE PORMENAZ" (2323m)
(return trip)

This route, which has become a classic in summer, is quiet in winter. Nic
views over the Fiz Mountains, the Diosaz valley and, of course, the Mor
Blanc.

- Map   : IGN TOP 25 ET Samoens
- Starting point   : Plateau d'Assy
- Height difference : 970 m
- Orientation   : south-east, then north
- Difficulty   : E-IMS
- Timing   : 3hrs30 - 4hrs up, 1 - 1hr30 down
- Time of year   : December-March

- **Itinerary** (photo 70)
  From the "Plaine Joux" carpark, go east under the "Teleski du Blaireau"
  Follow the road (cross-country ski tracks) to the "Chalets des Ayeres du
  Milieu", then those of the "Souay". Climb up left towards the "Fiz" mountain
  chain, then up right in the "Combe de l'Entrevie" (short, steep passage at the
  top). You find yourselves overlooking a gorge, which widens to form a small
  valley. Where the slope becomes less steep, go down rightwards into this valley and then climb up, more or less directly, the north face of the "Pointe Noir
  de Pormenaz" (succession of gullies cut through by rock barriers). Up the
  north-east ridge (on foot near the end) to the summit.

- **Descent:** Same way down.

- **Variation**
  You can also descend directly, on steep slopes, to the "Lac de Pormenaz".
  From the lake work left, and ski down the "Couloir de la Chorde" (35°),
  which brings you, after a short climb, to under the Chalets du Souay.

- **Safety tips**
  The Gorge du Souay is very narrow, with a steep passage and a high avalanche risk, we don't advise it.

→

Photo 70:
82. Pointe Noire de Pormenaz

Pointe Noire
de Pormenaz

82

LES CONTAMINES - SAINT-GERVAIS

CHAMONIX - MONT-BLANC

ARGENTIÈRE - LE TOUR

VALAIS (Swiss)

VAL D'AOSTE (ITALY)

THE AIGUILLES ROUGES

Bureau des Guides
et Accompagnateurs
des Contamines montjoie

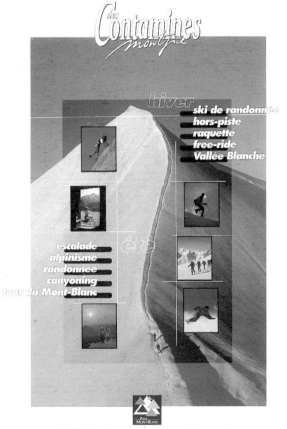

hiver

- ski de randonnée
- hors-piste
- raquette
- free-ride
- Vallée Blanche

été

- escalade
- alpinisme
- randonnée
- canyoning
- tour du Mont-Blanc

PAYS MONT BLANC

B.P. 29 - Les Contamines Montjoie
Tél. 04 50 47 10 08 - Fax 04 50 47 19 49